A Course Of Lectures On Drawing, Painting, And Engraving

William Marshall Craig

A

COURSE OF LECTURES

ON

DRAWING, PAINTING,

AND

ENGRAVING,

CONSIDERED AS

BRANCHES OF ELEGANT EDUCATION.

DELIVERED IN THE SALOON OF THE ROYAL INSTITUTION,

IN SUCCESSIVE SEASONS, AND

READ SUBSEQUENTLY AT THE RUSSELL INSTITUTION,

By W. M. CRAIG,

PAINTER TO HIS ROYAL HIGHNESS THE DUKE OF YORK.

Chi ben commincia ha la meta dell' opera.   GUARINI.

LONDON:

PRINTED FOR LONGMAN, HURST, REES, ORME, AND BROWN,

PATERNOSTER-ROW.

1821.

MANAGERS,

PROPRIETORS, AND SUBSCRIBERS,

TO THE

ROYAL INSTITUTION.

MY LORDS, LADIES, AND GENTLEMEN,

THE honour you did me by an unceasing and profound attention, during the delivery of those Lectures on Art which I was requested to prepare for you, will ever hold a gratifying place in my memory. The solicitations of many that I would publish them, encreased greatly the honour conferred upon me, and I have determined to yield to such wishes. The substance of my Lectures for nine seasons, are here consolidated and arranged; and I beg to ask for my publication, your kind and generous patronage, being,

My Lords,

Ladies and Gentlemen,

Your very obedient

and devoted servant,

W. M. CRAIG.

124. *Oxford Street,*
January 1. 1822.

INTRODUCTION.

IT has been frequently remarked, that scientific men write on their respective subjects, as if they were addressing each other only, and that their style is, in consequence, too technical or too elevated for those who wish to learn. But the duty which devolved upon me, of delivering a course of lectures to a mixed, though enlightened auditory, rendered circumspection upon this point exceedingly important. I had to address many who were already practitioners in elegant arts, yet who might

not have gone deeply into their principles;
I had to make myself intelligible to others
who had, probably, never before thought
on such subjects, and who might, perhaps,
be inclined to adopt them amongst the
number of their pursuits, by an apparent
facility in understanding ; and in addition,
I had to soothe my hearers, in order to induce them to remain with me to the end.
If in my endeavours for the attainment of
these objects, I have been too familiar, it
is an error on the side of usefulness ; if I
have sometimes been too florid, I trust it
has not been at the expence of elegance.
My mind was from the first most powerfully impressed with the important consequences that might result, from leading
such an audience to examine and imbibe,
the principles on which all the practices
of imitative art ought to be conducted.

Patronage is the proper nutriment of arts, but it should be patronage founded on solid common sense, and on feelings refined by contemplation; or, like deleterious food, it will excite bad habits, and unwholesome usages, in those who receive it. He, therefore, who endeavours on such subjects, to form the judgments of those, who by their rank or opulence, are destined to be the patrons of imitative art, is essentially serving its professors, he is rendering an important benefit to the country. An artist may labour for years, and without ceasing to produce works of real excellence; but it is all in vain, unless he find persons qualified to appreciate his powers; and, on the other hand, when youthful talent begins to show its dawnings, the well-informed patron may greatly assist to guide and direct its course, till it arrive at meridian splendour.

These considerations led me to undertake reading a course of lectures at the Royal Institution, as was suggested to me by a distinguished nobleman, then one of the committee of managers. The success which appeared to attend my endeavour in nine following seasons of that establishment, induced me to extend the same benefit to all who may wish for it by a printed publication of those lectures. If I should be regarded by some as the advocate of a mode, respecting which there are conflicting opinions, I beg to say, that I have not become so, without first giving a most serious and devoted attention to the subject, nor without offering indisputable facts and demonstrations, as to the truth of what I have thought it my duty to assert.

I beg to recommend the perusal of this work to my brother professors, though it is written principally for the information of a different class of persons, because I believe it will give them some new ideas and principles, and from other principles, which are not new to them, it will draw inferences that have probably not presented themselves before. I strongly advise my brethren, to encourage the practical study of these arts, amongst the opulent *dilettanti* of our country, for the reasons which I have stated already, and because their superiority in general education will soon requite the professors with superabundant assistance, in the results of contemplation and knowledge.

LECTURE I.

THAT a high state of the elegant arts in any country, is indicative of great advancement in civilization, has been so often asserted and proved, that we have no reasonable ground to deny the position. But it is important to our proposed discussions, to show that there is, in this case, a mutually reflected action, which, continually operating, produces consequences highly beneficial to the best interests of society. When a nation has passed through the agricultural state, in

B

which surplus produce is exchanged for
handicraft dexterity, and through those
dawnings of barter and commerce, which
result from a multiplied stock of manufactures of principal necessity, the most
successful individuals find they have more
property than their mere wants require,
and turn their thoughts to some new and
gratifying way of employing the accumulation.   In this state, merely as it results
from a surplus of property, the consequences have generally been, large halls,
sumptuous tables, and riotous feasts ; or,
under the influence of monkish supersti-
tion, such surplus has extended itself in
the dedication of extensive lands, and
funds for the support of supposed reli-
gious institutions ; but whenever the liter-
ature of accumulated ages beams on this
state of property, then the MIND begins to

examine its properties, begins to calculate
the means of its gratifications, and is
ready to offer substantial property for that
which is intellectual. From this period,
or state, in society, commences the progress of elegant·arts, in a continual interchange of invention and patronage, till
a superabundance of accumulated wealth,
and of patronage, arising from wealth, at
last seems to require that elegant arts
should be at the highest state of advancement, presuming the assiduity on one
side to be commensurate with the encouragement on the other ; but this progres-
sion, which takes place in every nation, is
observable, also, in the mass of nations
which form the great human society : and
then comes the collision of states, equally,
or almost equally, advanced in elegant
arts, which of them shall furnish, by su-

periority of tasteful fabrications, the greatest inducement to speculative demand.

In this state was Britain thirty years ago. — Equal in almost every manufacture to every other country, and in many superior; and soon after, our commerce became so improved, by the assistance of our advancement in the fine arts, that our enlightened statesman and financier, Mr. Pitt, thought it right to acknowledge this benefit, by exempting from a triplicate of the assessed taxes the principal professors of painting and sculpture.

Since that portentuous period, the wealth of our happy country has greatly increased, and peace with victory have, at length, intertwined their verdant wreaths around the dignified forehead of distinguished Britain. But in this new state, after half a century of sanguinary warfare, during which we monopolized the commerce of the world, we shall have to contend with the revived commercial talents of foreign nations ; and it, therefore, becomes a serious duty to every one amongst us, to examine what is the state of arts, and what may conduce most effectually to the improvement of that state. In such case, every one must do his part, and he must, and will do it, yea, zealously and faithfully, if he loves his country. That which I undertake, is to discuss before you the principles and practices of of drawing, painting, and engraving, so far as you are likely to engage in them, that you may qualify yourselves to become the judicious patrons of such as exercise those arts for their subsistence, and for the glory of their native land.

The plan I propose for this morning's lecture, is to give you a brief history of the three arts, with a view to point out, comparatively, their present state. I shall proceed, in my subsequent discourses, to examine the fundamental principles which each of them has in common with the others; to distinguish the principles that are appropriate to each; and from all *these*, to deduce such rules for practice, as shall lead, if rightly pursued, to the best results that have been obtained, by the most eminent practitioners, up to the present time. In this pursuit, I shall be led to examine the mental qualifications that are necessary to the professors of each art, in order to ensure success. I shall be led to point out, what appear to me, the mistakes of some, and the misrepresentations of others on these subjects ; I shall be led, inevitably, to point out the great advantages which arise from the cultivation of these arts to the individuals who study them, to the nations which take them under their most solemn protection.

I shall begin with Drawing, as the first in priority of existence, as the first element of the other two. Drawing, strictly speaking, is the art of representing objects by lines, which describe their contours or dimensions. It may be taken from the simple meaning of the word to draw, to pull out, or to produce in a line. The first drawings of the old masters were consonant to this idea, being nothing but a few lines made with a pen, or other pointed implement, to express the first conceptions of their minds on any subject. Thus, then, our verb, to draw, coincides

with the strict signification of the Italian
verb, " desegnare," and of the corre-
sponding French verb, " dessiner;" that
is, to express the first sentiment, or idea,
of the mind, which must be of forms only.
But the French, in many things the most
licentious of nations, and, in this instance,
the English thoughtlessly imitating them,
have allowed a latitude to this term,
which extends it greatly beyond its original and proper signification. The
meaning of words, it cannot be denied, is
a matter of custom and general consent;
yet if we were to fall without effort at
resistance, into every deviation that can
be made from first meanings, language
would soon lose its standard and utility,
by becoming unintelligible, except in
very small circles. We will, therefore,
attempt a compromise on the present oc-

casion, allowing as much as may be consistently allowed, to the licence of modern diction. Drawing, then, under this allowance, is the art of expressing the forms of natural objects by lines, with such additional aids from crayons, water-colours, or other materials, as tend to complete the indications of forms, without intending perfect resemblance. This is the ground on which the term, drawing, must stand, as applied to the present times ; but, when treading on the classical ground of antiquity, we must limit it to its first signification ; which the Italians have preserved to this day.

That drawing was practised before painting, or the use of colours, might be admitted, from its extreme probability, were there no facts to support the opinion ; but it appears, from various authorities, that the expressing or representing objects by lines, is of the highest antiquity.

That the earliest attempts of the Greeks were mere outlines, is certain, though learned authors differ as to the first practitioner ; and that even at the time when their painting was said to be at its highest perfection, they considered drawing, or outline, as the most essential quality, is evident from the anecdote given by Pliny of the visit paid by Apelles to Protogenès at Rhodes. The narrator, himself, declares to have seen the canvass on which this trial of skill took place, and describes it as exhibiting nothing more than a few simple lines. When the arts began to revive in Italy, the practice of painting, if it may properly be so called at that time, consisted of little more than outline. * Colours, it is true, were given to the masses of objects; but the outline was always most laboriously preserved by narrow shadows passing along its progress, and following its inflections. This manner is observable, also, at a later period, in the pictures of the Bellini, of Perugino, of Andrea del Sarto, and even in the early pictures of the incomparable Raphael Sanzio da Urbino. All these masters, too, made drawings of their first

* When Giotto, the pupil of Cimabue, was applied to for the purpose of getting him to paint for the then reigning pope, the emissaries employed on the occasion, questioned him as to his skill, requiring a specimen. He immediately drew a perfect circle with one motion of his hand, by which they were satisfied, and engaged him. This is a fair elucidation of the contest of manual dexterity between Apelles and Protogenès, which Hogarth and others have endeavoured to swell into a discussion of abstract principle.

thoughts, generally with a pen, previous to any attempt to paint a subject; and even the large studies in distemper, which they made on combined sheets * of paper, for their fresco pictures, may be, with few exceptions, considered as drawings; for in most of them the outline predominates, and is the first thing that strikes the eye. It has been subsequently the practice of almost every great master to accustom himself to drawing, as the proper means to acquire the true knowledge of forms. The portfolios of the dilletanti in this country, are filled with genuine specimens of this kind, by the hands of those whose finished works we reverence; but their several manners of process are not all suited for your adop-

---

* They are called cartoons, from cartone, a large paper, the Italian augmentative of carta, paper.

tion; of such as I conceive most eligible, I shall, on a future morning, offer you examples.

In Britain, the practice of drawing seems to have been introduced very early, though it was probably confined to the monks, who, for many centuries, were almost the sole possessors and preservers of every kind of knowledge.

The library of the British Museum has a curious folio volume, embellished with figures and other devices, executed in the reign of the great Alfred : the figures are in general faintly tinted with transparent water colours ; but the outline, which gives all the character and expression they have, is drawn very thick and dark with a pen. From that time, the practice of drawing seems to have disappeared in Britain, with few exceptions,

till the beginning of the last century.
In the reign of Henry the Eighth, however, we learn that Zucchero made two
drawings in Indian ·ink, after Holbein,
which are now in the collection of the
Honorable Mrs. Damer ; and these might
probably have led to the use of that
material as a pigment, since become so
general. The time allotted to this lecture
does not permit me to notice the drawings of Hayman, and some others, which
were produced a century or more after the
period I have just mentioned : they are
humble copies of the then prevailing style
of the French school, which was, at best,
but a bad imitation of the manner of
Carlo Maratti, by no means the most
eminent of Italian painters.   I pass these
over, because I must hasten to notice the
mode of drawing adopted and brought

into activity, nearly sixty years ago, by
Mr. Sandby.   In this process, the objects
were all drawn and strongly characterised
with a pen and Indian ink, the shadows
faintly inserted with the same material,
and the objects then thinly washed over
with indications of their local colours.
The outline of the pen was always left
evident, as the cause of expression; and
Mr. Sandby, in the precision and correctness of his enlightened mind, denominated
this manner tinted drawing, because of
the tints that were added to the outline.
But as the utmost stretch of this process
led to nothing more than what should
be called a sketch, succeeding artists made
additions to it, abandoning evident outline for the increasing force of darker
shadows and more powerful colours than
had been admitted before, till the result

has at last astonished and delighted every one. But the rapid advance, so recently made, has not allowed the public time to distinguish the necessity of applying the proper denomination to this new style. Because drawings have, in the last two centuries, been almost universally executed on paper, and because Mr. Sandby's ingenuity has led gradually to the most vigorous use of water colours on the same kind of surface, it has become a very general custom to call every thing drawing that is performed on paper with those materials, though the same persons who thus misuse the term, scruple not to apply the word *painting* to the very same process when exercised on ivory or on vellum. Let us, then, in order to avoid this error, let us keep in mind, that drawing, in its proper signification, means the art of representing the forms of objects by lines ; and, in its utmost latitude, can signify no more than the representation of objects by lines, with such additions from water colours, crayons, or other materials, as serve to complete the indication of forms, without aiming at complete imitation or deception.

Painting, the most difficult, the most comprehensive, and most sublime of all arts, is that of representing the true appearance of natural or possible objects by colours. The endeavour to ascertain when the art of painting was invented, or where it was first practised, is more likely to gratify the eagerness of the antiquary, to whose province it belongs, than to give information that would promote the improvement of the art in future. As such, it is not my wish to give you more than

c

a cursory view of this part of my subject, such as it results to my mind from a comparison of the best authorities I have been able to collect respecting it. It seems more than probable, that the existence of sculpture, even in round figures, was anterior to that of painting; because, as man's disposition is decidedly imitative, it would rather occur to him to represent round objects in their real dimensions, by labour, on some practicable material that might give equal rotundity, than to attempt it by the display of lines and colours on a flat surface. This opinion is authorised by the fact of some rude kind of sculpture being exercised amongst the most uncivilised islanders of the South Sea, where the use of lines or colours appeared to be totally unknown. But the practice of sculpture may be traced, with great appearance of probability, to a very early period in the antediluvian world; and the practice of painting, if we would suffer ourselves to be misled by some learned writers, who allow too great latitude to the term *picture*, might be carried up to the time of Enos, the son of Seth, and grandson of Adam. He, as learned rabbins maintain, seeing the descendants of Cain devote themselves to idolatry, endeavoured to lead them back to the true worship by representations on the sides of the altars, of figures of animals and other natural objects, to which he attached certain mystical significations; and thus, while the eye was amused, took occasion to inculcate, from the figures, the most sublime doctrine. It will however appear, I think, on a candid investigation, that the term picture was originally

employed to describe all representations
of objects on a flat surface, and that the
works of Enos, to which I have just al-
luded, were a species of outlines sculptured on some plain material, and afterwards filled up with colour.   This seems
to have been a very general practice
amongst the tribes who composed the
first kingdoms of the world, as there are
traces of it to be found in almost every
history; but we come to something like
a dawn of light on the subject of painting,
in looking on the fact, that the children
of Israel, in their long journey through
the wilderness, had an ensign or standard,
distinguished with appropriate figures, carried before each tribe.   It is true these
figures, in their various colours, might be
worked in embroidery; but even that, to
my mind, implies the previous existence

of some species of painting, which remark
may also be applied to the beautiful tapestry which Homer describes to have been
wrought by the fair hand of the bewitch-
ing Helen : for, even in these times, when
mechanic arts are carried to a degree of
perfection unknown before, all tapestry is
executed from a coloured or painted pattern. Leaving, however, the field of conjecture and mere probability, we arrive at
a fixed point to rest on, — though gloomy
be the situation, — it is in the catacombs
and sepulchres of the ancient Egyptians.
The early inhabitants of that country had
a practice of painting, in curious devices
and figures, the coffins destined for the
dead : many of these were not only painted
and finished in various colours, but were
also partially gilt ; and all this, by means
so durable, as to continue uninjured down

c 3

to modern times. That these were of great antiquity, cannot be doubted; for nothing of the kind is likely to have been performed there after the expedition of Cambyses into Egypt, who, according to Herodotus, enforced the adoption of his own manners and customs; to effect which more completely, he put to death the whole priesthood of the conquered country. We turn, then, our anxious eyes to the Greeks, who borrowed most of their arts from Egypt, and we find that the first who had any claims to the title of painter was Cleophantus of Corinth : he filled up the spaces inclosed by the outlines, which were generally made before, with one colour. Further advances were soon afterwards made by Cimon the Cleonœan, who added to the flat colour of his predecessors, a few lines to express the joints of the limbs and the appearance of folds in the draperies. In what century of the world these masters lived, is not at this time known; but we learn that, about the year 750 before Christ, the paintings of the Greeks were in such estimation that Candaules, king of Lydia, gave its weight in gold for one painted by Bularchus. From this time, during a period of more than four hundred years, the art continued to improve under the guidance of a succession of masters down to the time of Apelles, in whom the painting of the Greeks seems to have reached its highest point of excellence. In the last seventy or eighty years of this time, we find all the names of those great masters whom Pliny, and afterwards Pausanias, extolled to the utmost extent of the powers of language, as having produced works truly incomparable, and even miraculous. These writers, however, almost the only authorities we have on which to form an opinion of Grecian painting, these writers acquaint us, that the highly celebrated Zeuxis was generally censured for making the heads and the joints of his figures too large, as well as for not being able to give the proper expression and deportment to his personages ; and that Aristides, who lived contemporary with Apelles, *the prince of painters*, was the first artist who found a way to express the passions of the mind in the countenances of his figures. I wish to impress these facts upon your mind, as data from which, in another lecture, we shall have occasion to draw very important conclusions.

It is not necessary that I should trouble

you with a list of artists, generally inferior, who succeeded those I have mentioned; the most worthy will be separately spoken of, most probably, hereafter, where their particular merits apply to the points in discussion. I wish at present, in this brief history, merely to bring in review before you such leading events as influenced the destinies of the art. The dissensions and quarrels which took place amongst the successors of Alexander the Great, were unfavourable to the advancement of painting, and finally contributed to transfer the mysteries and practices of the Greeks, in this art, to the proud capital of the Roman empire ; for, after Paulus Æmilius had overcome Perseus, king of Macedon, he desired the Athenians to send him a skilful painter to adorn his triumph, and they unanimously

chose Metrodorus for this employment,
as the most celebrated artist of his time.
Rome, soon after this period, produced
some eminent painters, natives of her own
soil; and there can be no doubt that,
under the first emperors, the art flourished
in a high degree; for it was thought so
honourable an employment, that several
of those masters of the world took delight,
as we are told, in practising it, and even
excelled beyond many of their professors.
The tyrannies, the revolutions, the mas-
sacres, which marked the decline of the
Roman empire, were fatal to the progress
of taste in letters and in the arts; and the
clouds of northern barbarism, which collected in succession over the venerated
seats of learning and refinement, over the
whole extent of the civilised world, formed
a chaotic darkness, which the searching

eye of history has not always been able to penetrate. The faint traces of intellectual intelligence, of any kind, discoverable in this gloom of ages, are but like the thin ghosts that glide at midnight round the receptacles of the dead, making the desolation more dismal.

It is difficult to look on this change of the character of a great empire, from the most refined, the most learned, and the most voluptuous, to a state of the most savage barbarism, without making serious reflections on the nature and history of man, as it furnishes a subject of deep investigation to the moralist, as it exhibits an awful lesson to the rulers of kingdoms : but such reflections come not properly within the province of a lecturer on *imitative art*. The first dawn of light that beams on the history of painting, after this long

obscurity, is in the contest between the
emperors and the popes, whether pictures
should or should not be admitted in
churches and other places of worship. In
the course of this dispute, Pope Paul the
First, countenanced by the empress Irene,
called together the second council of Nice,
which decreed that pictures may be introduced in such places, and ordered the
restoration of all such as had been pulled
down by order of the emperor Leo Isau-
rus. Some of the distinctions, on this
subject, made by so learned an assembly,
are exceedingly curious, and may possibly
be mentioned hereafter in a lecture to
which they more properly belong; but I
must state to you, at present, that the
general result of these discussions was to
adopt painting as the same kind of auxiliary to the Catholic religion which sculp-

ture had been, for many ages before, to the worship of Pagan deities. The paintings, if such they should be called, of this period, and even for a long time afterwards, were all executed by Greek artists, who travelled to different parts of Europe, when required, to exercise their calling round the altars of the true God. There is much reason to believe that these itinerant workmen had a certain set of designs, or rather patterns, handed down from generation to generation, from which they never ventured to deviate even in a single line. They were doubtless *such* as we see, though smaller, in the worst of the painted missals which now remain to us, and were probably much inferior to the paintings of the Chinese of this time. They were little more than flat masses of glaring colours, divided into shapes by

strong lines, and were very frequently
heightened on each colour with gilding.
This was the state of painting in the middle of the thirteenth century, when the
city of Florence had the honour of giving
birth to one who raised this sublime art
from its degraded, mechanical state, by
recurring to its true object, which is *na-*
ture, and he is very properly called the
father of modern painting. Cimabue was
of noble parents, and, being destined by
them for one of the learned professions,
as they are called, he received, in consequence, such an education as falls to the
lot of few painters in these times, but
which, no doubt, most powerfully aided
his efforts, when allowed to indulge the
prevailing disposition of his mind, that
had early manifested itself in favour of
painting. He is said to have been the

inventor of painting in fresco, which he
applied to decorate the outsides of houses
and other buildings ; though I am inclined
to think him not entitled to the praise of
this discovery, for he received his knowledge of the process of painting from some
Greeks that were then employed at Florence in decorating the church of Santa
Maria Novella, who doubtless possessed
amongst them, by regular descent, the
secrets of ancient art with regard to materials, though they had lost every par-
ticle of the science which had before so
nobly employed them. That painting in
fresco was known to the ancients, I cannot hesitate to believe ; for the pictures
of the Greeks were frequently executed,
and, to remain in open places, exposed
to the weather ; and we find that, in the
reign of Augustus Cæsar, one Ludius,

the reputed inventor of landscape painting, executed various kinds of landscape
scenery on the fronts of public buildings,
for which purpose the nature of distemper
colours, commonly used by the ancients,
would have been highly improper. In further corroboration of this opinion, I have
to state to you, that some of the ancient
paintings, lately dug up from the ruins of
Herculaneum, appear to be executed in
fresco. But, returning from this digression, we see the practice of painting im-
proving by the exertions of successive
practitioners, who pursued the path which
Cimabue had pointed out, down to the
time of Raphael, Corregio, and Titian,
who collectively displayed, in a pre-emi-
nent degree, every excellence of which
this art is capable. That painting, at this
period, was in a higher state of improve-

ment than it had ever been before, I dare
venture to affirm, without the fear of
misleading you, though not without the
risk of contradiction ; that this highly improved state of painting has never since
been equalled, is not now denied by any
one. On these points, however, I shall have
occasion to speak more fully on some other
morning. It is highly important, in the
history of this art, to observe, that, in
the time of those three great men, the
practice of painting in oil colours became
general, and gave to the artist some advantages which he did not possess before.
What was the real amount of these advantages, must remain for future discussion, in a comparison of the process of
painting in oil with that of painting in
water-colours, as at present understood:
it is a subject of very serious and im-

D

portant enquiry. From the time of Raphael, the art appears to have declined: grandeur of conception, in one school, gave way to splendour of colouring; truth of imitation, in *another*, made room for affected grandeur; and the broad simplicity, and tender outline of Corregio, disappeared almost every where. It is true, the declining art found a prop in the exertions of the Carracci, who appear great in comparison with their contemporaries, though inferior to the masters who adorned the century before them; yet their efforts, as well as those of Reubens and Vandyke, were unavailing; and this splendid art, which was born in Greece, and regenerated in Italy, made its last struggles for continued existence in Holland or in England. The practice of the French painters, during any part of this

period, I count for nothing, as they had
no influence on the progress of the art :
they are too insignificant to be mentioned
in so brief a history. This dignified,
this sublime art, which had hitherto been
employed in recording the miracles or
the sufferings of the incarnate Divinity,
and which might have recovered the temporary depression, was stopped short in
its dazzling career by the influence of
puritanic fanaticism, and forced to exert
its best energies in feeding the personal
vanity, as it has been called, or in decorating the apartments of the wealthy or the
ostentatious. The inducement was thence-
forth of a sordid nature, unlike the
glowing enthusiasm which operated before, and the direful consequences to the
art were soon manifested in its decline
to a state of comparative decrepitude.

The establishment of a national school, in the capital of these kingdoms, has opened a fair prospect for a second revival of painting; the benevolent and fostering care of majesty, has aided the undertaking; and the wealth of a generous and enlightened public, has been freely poured forth to second the glorious example. What further remains for this generous public to do, towards a consummation so devoutly to be wished, it will be my duty humbly to suggest, as the occasions may arise, in the course of these lectures. The unanimous and vigorous exertions of the professors, will then only be wanting to place the British school of painting in a rank not inferior to that of any school which has yet existed in other countries.

By engraving, I would be understood

to signify that art of representing natural objects, the ultimate purpose of which is to transfer the labour of the artist to paper, or some other material, by means of pressure. It is performed by incision, and the medium of transfer is delivered sometimes from the cavities, and sometimes from the projecting surface. Ingenious or learned men may allow a greater extent to the term, in order to show their erudition, or to give a seeming value to the art by reputed antiquity; but the general understanding of the word engraving, is what I wish to meet, and not to confound it with what more properly belongs to sculpture.

At what period this art was first practised is not certain: Vasari gives the first discovery to Fineguerra, a Florentine goldsmith, in the year 1460. It had

long been a practice to engrave ornamental devices of various kinds, on pieces
of plate, and also on clasps of gold and
silver, for the purpose of filling the
cavities with enamel, or with a different
coloured metal ; and it was usual to take
casts of these in earth, or in melted sul-
phur, to ascertain the progress of the
work, and its fitness for the purpose intended.   Fineguerra observed on these
occasions, that the parts of the cast which
came out of the incisions were discoloured and dark, and he conceived from
it the possibility of taking similar impressions with paper.   He tried, therefore,
with a plate of silver, which he engraved,
and to which he probably applied some
additional means of colouring the cavities.
On this he laid a moist paper, and
rubbed it over for some time with a

roller; so that, on taking the paper off the silver plate, it was not only embossed, but the lines appeared black, as if drawn with a pen. Such is the account given by Vasari, whose text, on the occasion, is not very perspicuous. Whether, in this case, he acted from the partiality which every man feels to the glory of his own country, or whether his knowledge on the subject was limited, we cannot now determine; but certain it is, that we have impressions on paper, from a plate of same kind of metal, engraved in Germany or Flanders, in the same year which is fixed on by Vasari for the discovery supposed to be made by the Florentine goldsmith; and, when we consider that the practice of painting in oils, supposed to be invented in Holland by Van-eych, was more than forty years travelling

into Italy, we can scarcely suppose the
other art should have passed over the
same distance in less than as many weeks.
The success of Fineguerra, induced Bal-
dini, another goldsmith of the same city,
to make further experiments, in which
he also succeeded ; but being himself no
draftsman, he procured assistance from
Sandro Botticelli, whose designs he generally engraved, thus laying the first
foundation for connecting the painter's
and the engraver's arts. Polaiolo, a celebrated anatomical draftsman of the same
period, executed some plates that display
a considerable improvement in the practice of engraving, and which excited the
attention of Andrea Mantegna, an ingenious painter, then at Rome, who applied
himself seriously to the new art, for the
purpose of engraving his own designs.

He carried the practice of engraving so much further than his predecessors, as to have obtained a great part of the praise which belongs to the first discovery: his plates of the triumphs of Julius Cæsar, were, probably, the first engravings that were generally circulated. Germany, at the same time, produced very able com-petitors to Mantegna, in Israel Martin and Il Tedesco, whose works were exe-cuted with great attention and labour, but whose greatest praise is that they communicated the practice of their art to the justly celebrated Albert Durer, to Aldegrave, and to Lucas Van Leyden, who soon became more eminent than their masters. The mind of Albert Durer seems to have been formed for the execu-tion of great designs in art, and had it not been restrained and shackled, by the

stiff, and, as it is called, Gothic style,
which at that time pervaded all the northern schools of painting, he might, probably, have proved a powerful rival to the
most eminent, in either profession. His
engravings in copper are characterised by
a degree of precision and truth, which is
astonishing *at this day*, when every possible trick in art is adopted to conceal a
want of finishing; but the labour and time
they required to execute them, proved a
fatiguing restraint on Durer's productive
mind, and he took to engraving his designs on wood, in which mode he was,
probably, the first who produced any thing
worth looking on. Some of these latter
performances being exposed for sale at
Venice, were seen by Mark Antonio Rai-
mondi, who thence resolved to make engraving his pursuit; and, being after-

wards chiefly employed in engraving the works of the incomparable Raphael Sanzio, became the greatest artist of his time in that profession. It ought not, however, to be said, that he possessed higher mechanical powers, as an engraver, than were possessed by Durer; but having constantly before his eyes, as sole objects of his study, the magical and fascinating works of so sublime a painter, the spirit of his original was necessarily transfused through his mind into the copper, which thence speaks a language that it could never have derived from Mark Antonio's unassisted efforts. From this time, the art of engraving gradually extended itself to every part of civilised Europe; and sometimes one, and sometimes another country, could boast of the most successful practitioners; but in all countries, and

in the works of all engravers, for a century
and a half, this characteristic feature is
observable, that, whatever picture or
drawing, or other original, were the object of imitation, the engraver copied
only the outline of his model, and a distinction of the different surfaces into
actual light and actual shadow, never
thinking to express those degrees of dark
and light which arise from difference of
local colour, or from recession in distance.
It remained for a person of high birth to
stimulate the professors of engraving to
a FURTHER exertion of their powers, by a
discovery which has highly benefited the
the world. Prince Rupert, amidst those
generous exertions in support of royalty
which render his name dear to every
Briton, found time to cultivate the arts,
and seeing a centinel one day cleaning

from his fusil a rust which the night-dew
had formed upon it, conceived the first
idea of a mode of engraving, since called
mezzotinto, from its expressing the middle tones or tints better than any other
process. There are three prints, from
plates by the hand of the prince, still to
be seen, with Evelyn's account of the discovery. This new mode did not, in its
own operations, produce all the good effects which its first admirers predicted;
but it served, by comparison, to shew the
other engravers what further was wanting
to their process, and even in this alone
the invention was highly important by its
effects. It became the study of engravers
in every nation, after this time, to express
the tones and texture of different objects,
as arising from difference of colour and
material; but the undertaking was so

novel, so comprehensive, and so difficult, that every one proceeded with timidity, and the progress was, therefore, gradual and slow. The French, even at this day, though the best engravers on the Continent, are very sparing in their endeavours to express these tones ; and it is no extravagant panegyric to say, that the English engravers, within these fifty years, have done more in this way than has been done before by the engravers of any other age or country.

I have endeavoured to be as brief as possible in this historical sketch of the three arts, and have taken only the most striking features, because I wish to impress them strongly on your minds. A critical examination of the various processes in each, with a view to ascertain their comparative merits, will furnish materials for subsequent discussions.

The influence of drawing, painting, and engraving, on the happiness and welfare of human society, is very considerable, and, perhaps, much greater than it has generally been supposed, unless by some of the most enlightened. They furnish the means of promoting, of multiplying, and of publishing mechanical inventions of every kind; they furnish the means of conveying to the utmost limits of the habitable world, the most valuable information, in any pursuit, and that too in a language which is instantly intelligible; a language which possesses a degree of clearness and precision that words can never reach; they may be made the sources of the most refined enjoyment, the soothers of sorrow, the monitors of vice, and the records of individual affection ; but, *above all*, these arts have been made the splendid means of exciting the heroes of Britain to new deeds of unparalleled daring, by publishing, to admiring and envying nations, their noble achievements, with a truth and feeling so lively, as scarcely to be equalled by the impression those achievements have left in the hearts of their grateful countrymen.

Drawing, taken merely as the art of representing forms by lines, is of high importance to every class in the community. The artisan, if he have the power thus of laying down his conception, will save himself much labour and time. The machinist, if he be a skilful draftsman, may try on paper, in a few hours, the most complicated union of mechanical principles, without subjecting his employers to those disappointments, and those losses, in which large fortunes have repeatedly been buried. The soldier and sailor will ever find a skill in drawing the most powerful aids, for ascertaining, with correctness and with promptitude, the truth of geographical situation. The man of taste, who travels, will, by this art, be enabled to impress forcibly on his memory, the interesting features, the beauties of other countries, and by them to embellish his own.

The art of painting, the universal language, stands on the highest pedestal in the temple of imitative arts: its operations, when complete, involve the most comprehensive knowledge, and its influence is great in proportion to the powers of intellect required in its performance. I shall not now speak of the exertions of

E

painting, when applied to portraiture, by
which balm has so often been poured
into the wounded breast, and the pangs
of temporary or final separation mitigated
to a soothing melancholy.   I will not now
speak of its exertions in landscape, by
which the transient effects of atmosphere,
or the ever-varying beauties of the seasons,
are fixed and perpetuated.   I will speak
of painting now, only as the means of
embodying the verbal representations of
past historians and poets, as the means
of transmitting to future ages the noble
actions of our contemporaries.

The ancient Greeks employed the powers
of sculpture to honour their gods, to
commemorate their heroes and great men;
though this art has nothing to boast, in
competition with painting, but its probably greater duration.   The sculptor, in

his representations, is confined to a small compass; in the first place, by the nature of his material; and again, by the necessity he is under of representing solid forms, and actual, not apparent, dimensions. On the other hand, painting can extend its surface at pleasure, can multiply its objects without control, can represent *truly*, almost every kind of object; and, in apparent distance, is confined only by the probable limits of vision. The sculptor is also greatly restricted in his means of expressing passion; he cannot even indicate the direction of the eye without violating the truth of his art; he cannot give the pallid hue of death, the glow of indignation, or the flush that tinges the cheek of offended modesty; whilst all these are among the least difficult operations of painting. We have a

remarkable instance of the great embarrassment which sculptors encounter, occasionally, in the famous pillar of Trajan.
The artist was required to represent, in
the series, one of the achievements
of that celebrated warrior, which was
performed during a violent storm of rain,
and has thus endeavoured to express
it: He has sculptured over the heads
of the combatants, a large head with
a long beard, and wide-spread, flaggy
wings, which is understood to represent
a Jupiter Pluvius. This, I conceive, bor-
ders, as nearly as any thing can, on the
burlesque in representation; while, in the
hands of a skilful painter, the circumstance of a band of intrepid warriors,
crossing a rapid river, and defeating a
host of savage foes, during an elementary
war, would produce one of the most sublime and most impressive combinations.

Thus, then, it is evident, that sculpture, on a comparison with painting, has but a very limited power, when applied to the purpose of recording historical events; and this country has, therefore, wisely given painting the preference to which it is so justly entitled. I trust, too, that a time will yet come, perhaps at no very distant period, when the cold inanimate piles of marble gods and goddesses, which have been built up in our Christian temples to honour the memories of Christian heroes, will give place to the splendid, life-giving representations of the pencil. The space they would occupy, would be considerably less, and they would have power to excite in the admiring spectator a more lively sympathy, a more generous emulation. I wish, most earnestly, to press this consi-

E 3

deration on the attention of those who
profess themselves the anxious friends
and promoters of our school of painting.
But when we look on this art as the
source from which the engraver must
draw all his materials to work on, and
take into view the extensive operation
and tendency of the two arts, acting in
conjunction, we must be struck, at once,
with their moral and political importance.

The British nation owes its security,
its independence, its prosperity, in a
great measure, to the unparalleled valour
of its heroic defenders ; and a new race
of heroes is continually preparing for the
glorious struggle, by the narratives and
the lively representations of what others
have achieved before them.

Painting, therefore, amongst the *great*,

and engraving amongst the *inferior classes*, will be the happy means of exciting this patriotic enthusiasm. Verbal description may do much in the statement of great events; but it must, from its nature, take the particular circumstances successively; and, in consequence, while one is relat- ing, another, which has been previously described, is losing its force on the mind. It requires many sentences, sometimes many pages, to relate the perils of a par- ticular achievement, and the magnani- mous resolution with which they were encountered; but a skilful representation of such events, in picture or in engrav- ing, gives every impressive particular to the spectator in an instant, and we know that those impressions are the most lively which are conveyed to the mind in the shortest space of time. Thus, then, engraving, as the means of multiplying and of circulating, at a comparatively small expence, those important excitements which painting has already effected at a much greater expence, must be looked on as a powerful instrument in promoting great national objects. If we take a view of engraving, in its lesser influences, we shall find them numerous, and still highly beneficial. Of these, I shall mention a few only, leaving the rest to be suggested by your deliberate reflection. Whoever wishes to form his mind to a correct taste for pictures, with the view either to make a collection of his own, or to enjoy the collections of others, will find it the best mode to begin by the study of prints. From these he will learn to know the different manners or styles that have cha-racterised different nations or schools, and the peculiarities that distinguish the various masters, even of the same school. This the dilletanti will be able soon to accomplish; because a great number of prints, occupying only a small space, can be brought into comparison with each other at a single view; and it would also be a matter of consideration to some, that a numerous collection of engravings for such purpose, may be made at an expence, not, perhaps, exceeding the price of one good picture. The student in history, who, unless possessed of a mind uncommonly retentive, must, necessarily, in time, lose a considerable part of what he reads, will be enabled by a well-chosen set of prints, to revive, in a few minutes, the perfect remembrance of what would cost him weeks, months, and even years, to renew by the means from which he

first imbibed it ; and this revival, by the
new association, leaves the impression
stronger even than at first. Thus, then,
a collection of engravings makes an important part of education. The naturalist,
in any department, must shut up his dis-
coveries in his own bosom, or trust them
to the vague and indefinite conveyance of
words, were it not for the pencil and the
graver ; but, aided by these means, he
conveys with undiminished accuracy, the
result of his most abstruse investigations,
to thousands, to millions ; and the collec-
tor of such engravings can hence form a
complete cabinet of natural history, in so
small a compass as not to be inconveni-
ent to a very limited establishment. The
lover of biographical reading, in accompanying his pursuit by a collection of
engraved portraits, gives a new and more

lively interest to every progressive step; he associates the character with the features of each individual, and they seem to form around him a circle of friends and intimate acquaintances. The man who pants for a knowledge of distant nations, but whom peculiar circumstances of situation deprive of the power to visit them, may, by a well-chosen collection of prints, possess himself, without personal risk or exertion, of all that information which the most laborious or enterprising travellers have brought from near or remote kingdoms and states; he may learn the figures, the countenances, the habits, and customs of the natives; he may view, at leisure and in safety, their various coasts, their rich plains, their extensive woods, their verdant or burning mountains; and he may even enter into a minute examination of their numerous productions in vegetable or animated life.

Such are the histories, such the pretensions of those three arts, which the interest of your country now calls on you to protect, to patronise, to cherish; and I dare believe that, to the minds, to the hearts of Britons, the calls of patriotism will never be uttered in vain.

LECTURE II.

———

DRAWING and painting have the same object in pursuit, with very different degrees of power, and the one may fairly be considered as the indispensable preparative for the other art. This object is the imitation of natural appearances, such as have actually existed, or such as might exist, all circumstances concurring to that end. This seems so evident, that the enquiring mind may be disposed to wonder that it should ever have been denied by any one, and it has been the professed

object of every great painter, down almost to the present time. But since the
position has been disputed, and that too,
in our own country, by an artist of distinction, living not many years ago, we
shall do well to examine the ground on
which such a negative is founded. The
French, always fanciful, and often frivo-
lous in arts and in sciences, first threw
out such an idea in their treatises of art,
but it remained for an Englishman to
assert it positively in public discussions.
This high authority maintained in his first
discourses, that general and not individual nature is to be imitated in drawing
and painting, and that abstract ideas are
what every great master in those arts is
bound to represent; and in his final essay
on this subject, he has unequivocally insisted that " painting is, strictly speaking,

no imitation at all of external nature."
There is a seeming contradiction in these
assertions, but they resolve themselves
into the same principle, under the inex-
plicable proposal of painting ideal nature
or ideal beauty. We will first examine
the terms, general and abstract, which on
this occasion, must be intended as syno-
nymous. Abstraction, as defined by Locke,
is a power of the mind to reject from its
simple ideas whatever belongs to, or
constitutes, a species of object or thing,
and to retain what each of a kind has in
common with others of the same kind.
The abstract idea, therefore, of a flower,
is not a rose, or a carnation, or a lily, or
a hyacinth; nor is it blue, or red, or yellow, or inclining to any of these; it has
neither form nor colour, nor altitude nor
dimensions, and yet it is a flower: again,

the abstract idea of a tree is neither black nor brown, nor green nor blue ; neither spreading nor perpendicular ; having foliage of no form or dimensions ; and having branches without form and bark, without colour or texture.   I adduce these instances, in *familiar* objects, to show the nature of abstract ideas,. which, if a power exist in the mind to form them, and it has been most ably denied by Dr. Ried and others, it is plain that such ideas are purely intellectual, and far beyond the cognizance of representative art.   It will not escape the distinct observation of an auditory like this, that whatsoever becomes an object of vision or sight, becomes immediately specific, and cannot be general.   To be *evident*, to be *tangible* by human sense, it must have distinct form ; it must have length and breadth; and it must have colour of some kind or other; all of which, when discernible, are no longer general or abstract. If we look for the elucidation of this *impracticable* practice, in the works of those who have been its chief advocates, we find the result of their reasons to be, the substitution of something for nature, which is not like nature, but which they have repeated and viewed with self-complacency, till they have really believed it to be what they call a representation of general, or abstract, or ideal nature ; though perfectly unintelligible to all who have not been used to their school and series of arbitrary indications. This may be compared to one who sits ruminating before the fire during the twilight of a winter's evening; and, fancying at last that he sees in various parts of the burning mass, mountains, trees, figures, and faces, calls his companions to look at the discovery, and finds they can trace no such resemblance. The vicious practices in art, which have resulted from these notions, in our own time, are many and grievous, because their tendency is to deny the legitimate object of pursuit, and to leave the student to his own wild fancies, without a criterion to judge of his exertions. But if this doctrine of painting abstract ideas, be supposed a misconception of the artist's duty to select objects, or parts of objects, for his imitation, then we may venture to treat it with more serious consideration. There are many objects in nature, that are, of themselves, unsightly and disagreeable ; there are many parts of objects in nature, which a countless variety of

accidents and habits may have altered
from their original design; and these circumstances are to be found; almost without exception; in every object that can
come before our sight. The student of
nature, therefore, when he shall have acquired a perfect facility in expressing
truly whatever he views, should; by close
observation and constant reasoning; accustom himself to reject accidental defects, and to restore to every object its
true proportion of possible beauty.

In a tree, in a rock that he may chance
to meet, the shape may have been distorted by a number of different causes ;
the quantity may happen to be greater or
less than he wishes it for the purposes of
picturesque effect ; yet, in making additions or deductions from one or the other,
a strict attention to his former studies

should prevent him from representing the rock or the tree other than would be evidently possible to such objects, under more favourable circumstances. The accidents that attend the human figure, the most important and the most difficult object of imitative art, are infinitely more numerous than those which befal the inanimate, or the brute creation; giving more latitude to the artist, and requiring deeper investigation. Man is not bound down by positive and unvarying laws of labour and rest, hunger and satiety, occurring in regular succession, and always producing the same consequences; his reason, which gives him a boasted superiority over other creatures, sets him at once above the instinct that leads them to the constant fulfilment of their destination, and makes him liable to a thousand chance impressions, arising from his caprice. The passions, the dispositions, the occupations of men, have all their respective influences on the countenance, the complexion, the limbs, and the general figure, often abating or increasing so much of the relative proportions of part to part, which goes a great way to constitute personal beauty.

It may very properly be asked, what rules, what principles there are to direct us in this rejection of the defects of nature, in this search after her genuine unadulterated beauties? Beauty, in visible objects, is that fitness of the parts to the end proposed by the whole; that happy combination of forms, that intricate and delicate association of tints, which excites in the human mind a sympathetic consciousness of its alliance to the great Author of all

perfection, of which beauty in all things
is the evident sign. In proportion, therefore, as the soul is enlightened and sub-
limed, in proportion as its powers become
enlarged by reflection, and purified by a
love of virtue, so will be its approxim-
ation to the ultimate perfection, and so
its sympathetic perception of visible beauty. On this principle, we shall be enabled readily to account for the variety of
opinions entertained by the people of different nations, with regard to personal
beauty in men or women. The savages
of Africa, and of the South Sea islands,
sunk in that ignorance which makes
them, in mind, little better than the
brutes that howl around them, not only
doat on the species of human form which
their country presents to them, but even
seem, in many instances, to think it still

more admirable when maimed and distorted. The Chinese, though considerably refined beyond most nations of the
East, are remarkable for many prejudices
of this kind, as we may justly infer from
the countenances and figures they give,
in painting, to their most favourite deities.

Amongst the various states of Europe,
where civilization and science have made
great advances, and where, of course, the
human mind is raised nearer to that perfection of which it is capable, the difference of sentiment in each nation, with regard to personal beauty, is much diminished, by all approaching the same point.
On this principle may be solved also the
difficulty which has puzzled some of the
learned essayists on these subjects, respecting the share that novelty has in promoting the pleasure we derive from the

F 4

contemplation of beauty. These essayists, in the pride of philosophy, attributing every thing to matter and to man, involve themselves and their followers in embarrassments, because they will not look up for elucidations of the actions of *mind*, to that celestial fountain from which mind began, and by which it continues. It is certainly true, as they state, that whatever is beautiful in itself, is beautiful in the same degree, though looked at and regarded for millions of times, if such a thing should be possible by the same individual ; but it is also as true, that the most perfect objects lose a portion of their power to excite interest in the spectator, by being repeatedly contemplated. This is so well known, that it is almost come to a proverb : the poet says,

Beauty soon grows familiar to the lover,
Fades on the eye, and palls upon the sense;

and if it thus lose its charm to him who
has begun with doating upon it, what
must be its still more transient influence
on those in whose admiration passion has
no share. The kind of philosophers to
whom I allude, charge this versatility on
the depravity of man's habits, on his want
of cultivated mind; but the truth appears
to be, that when the *mind* is elevated to
a tolerable perception of beauty, it has
made so much advance towards the nature
and source of its being ; and, having compared and examined sympathetically, such
indications of divine perfection, it pants
in its state of progress for new and greater
demonstrations. To illustrate this, we
will refer to common experience. There
are some men, and many females, in this
land of beauty, whose limbs, proportions,
and features, are so perfect, that the most

judicious statuary would think himself
fortunate in being able to copy them;
they have, also, we will allow, all the advantages of complexion; yet these moving
statues, it is known, are looked at, contemplated, admired, and forgotten; for
all their properties are properties of matter only, though indicating the skill and
power of the great Artificer. Let us look
next to others whom we know, who possess no exact proportion of limb, no peculiar symmetry of feature, no uncommon
advantage of complexion; yet we all have
experienced that such persons, if irradi-
ated by minds highly sublimated, seem
lovely, seem beautiful, are followed with
eagerness, are left with regret, and are
always and for ever anxiously desired. It
is evident that the qualities which produce
such permanent effects, being qualities
above matter, produce them by that al-

liance which is immediately acknowledged between spiritual essences emanating from the same fountain of ineffable perfection.

But returning from the digression, by this perpetual selection and study of the perfect parts of individual objects, the practitioner in painting, stores his mind with perfect images of every class in nature, which he can draw forth for the purposes of his art, whenever occasion shall require it. Yet these images are not generalizations of realities; they are perfect individuals, which might have existed in nature, though, perhaps, they never did. The fallacious theory which I have endeavoured to expose leads, on the contrary, to a random manner of drawing and painting, decidedly abridging the art as a universal language, but which has, however, this advantage, as declared by

one of its public advocates, that its results, if they be not like what they are
intended for, may easily be mistaken for
something else.*   But that the legitimate
object of painting is to imitate external
nature, we have the evident authority of
all the *great* masters, who have lived either
in ancient or modern times, with the
strange exceptions I have mentioned already.   It will be well to review these instances.   Apelles, the most celebrated
painter of the Greeks, became enraged
with his much-laboured picture of Alexander the Great, on his famous Bu-
cephalus, because he could not express
the foam from the horse's mouth.   He
threw his sponge at the picture, which,
happening to strike precisely on the part
in which the artist had failed, produced

---

* See Gilpin on the Wye.

the imitation he wished for, but could not accomplish; and the picture was finished and preserved. In the contest of comparative talent between Zeuxis and Parrhasius, of nearly the same period, the first brought to the trial, as a proof of his highest skill, a bunch of grapes which he had painted, and considered himself secure of triumph, because his *imitation* was so correct that birds had attempted to eat the fruit while exposed to view. Parrhasius's tablet presented a curtain, which he declared concealed the efforts of his skill, which Zeuxis, trying to withdraw, found it was only a painted curtain, and owned himself vanquished. We draw two important conclusions from these circumstances. The first is, that the highest class of Grecian painters considered the perfect imitation of nature as the very essence of their art; and the second conclusion is, that all of them had not arrived at such power of imitation. I am prepared to show, in a subsequent Lecture, that the painting of the ancient Greeks never was carried beyond this point.

When the judicious practices of this art, as well as of other arts, died away, perhaps, in some measure, owing to want of study, and the consequent want of knowledge in the professors, nature was gradually neglected, and at last wholly forsaken. Such, and from such causes, was the miserable state of painting amongst the Greeks, in the middle of the thirteenth century. To paint a head, or figure from the life, was, at that time, considered miraculous; but the genius of Cimabue saw, though perhaps faintly, that painting must be an imitative art, or it can be nothing good, on which account he studied most of his heads, some of his whole figures, and many of his draperies, from nature; and thus; in a short time, completely surpassed the Greeks who had first instructed him. His pupil, Giotto, carried the art many degrees further, by adopting the same principle : and, nearly two hundred years afterwards, we find the great, the learned, the incomparable Da Vinci*, proving, both by his works, and by the most philosophical discussions, that there is no way to excellence in painting, but by an incessant study of nature. The immortal Raphael knew so well the importance of studying and imitating nature closely, that, besides making many drawings from the natural, of any object which he meant afterwards

* I recommend, most earnestly, to perusal of every one who may meet with it, the " Trattato della pittura," of this master.

to paint, he frequently added the further labour of modelling his objects in clay, so as to understand every part of them before he took up the pencil. Rubens, who shines deservedly the brightest star among the painters of the north, though he had seen and studied during some years, the great works of art at that time to be found in Italy, chose rather to copy the clumsy and vulgar nature, which, after his return, his own country set before him, than to run the risk of a deviation from truth, by trusting to his imagination or his memory. It is through the medium of this principle, also, that we must look at the productions of the Dutch painters, whose works are sought for with eagerness by every person of taste, solely on account of the exquisite skill and truth with which the imitation of nature is rendered. You are well acquainted with those names that stand so high in the Dutch and Flemish schools for this kind of excellence, and the inference to be drawn from them is obvious.

Thus, then, I trust, it appears that painting, as ·an imitative art, has a fixed and determinate object; and that any attempt to carry its practices beyond the highest possible degree of selection, must be a romantic scheme, which leaves serious judgment on the earth astonished, and carries imagination, like an air-balloon, out of the reach of human cognizance, to float, or fly, as it may please the aeronaut who inflated it. The result of these various observations will be, that, while I recommend at first, the most rigid imitation of objects, as they are presented to us, for the purpose of storing

the mind with accurate ideas, and of acquiring facility of true execution in the
hand, the end of such preparation will
be a disposition to reject, in your subsequent representations, the accidents which
deteriorate the perfections of natural objects. You will then be aware that it is
not every thing we see, or every combination presented to us, that will make an
interesting picture; elegance of form may
be wanting in one, contrast, or harmony
of colours, in another, and, perhaps, appropriate light and shadow in a third;
but you will be disposed to insist, that
where form, colour, and breadth of shadow, such as an artist would wish for his
picture, are combined in the scene or
group offered to his view, the artist who
imitates most closely every thing in it dis-
cernable, from the point at which he is

supposed to stand, will make the best picture. I trust it may now be allowed, that I have satisfactorily shewn that painting can have no other object than to imitate nature. It is, therefore, of importance, next to examine the means which we possess for accomplishing this desirable purpose. The materials of this art are black and white pigments, as the extremes of power, with red, blue, and yellow, and their modifications and combinations: these are intended to be applied on a flat surface, in order to represent near or distant forms, prominent objects, and cavities ; and the wanton daring of self-complacent professors, has often employed them in the endeavour to represent luminous bodies. But we shall soon find that the powers of this art are extremely limited and deficient, even with a view to the contracted purposes to which I would confine its operations.

To prove this, we will suppose a bust, or statue, of white marble, or plaster of Paris, to be placed in the shadowy part of a room, and a picture painted of it in the same room, with the lights as bright, and the shadows nearly as dark as they appear in nature : the marble or plaster being pure white, the highest lights in the picture must be pure white also. Remove the picture and the figure into strong sunshine, and the highest lights of both will become much more brilliant; but the darkest shadows on the figure will remain nearly as dark as before, while those in the picture will appear much lighter ; and it will, of course, when compared with its original, seem faint and flat, though the shadows be painted as dark as art can

make them. ·I will propose another case
for your consideration. We see a venerable hermit sitting, in the full glow of
noontide brightness, at the entrance of his
cell, which is no more than the deep hollow of some shattered rock; he is holding
his book full in the sun, that his aged
eyes may distinguish the characters he
wishes to read. You are struck with the
combination, and sit down, with all your
implements and materials, to paint the
whole scene. You begin with the figure,
and you find it necessary to employ your
purest white to represent the dazzling
light on his book, and the shine on his
beard and silver hairs. In the whole of
this, however, you succeed completely;
for your imitation receives the same intense light as the objects themselves. Delighted, you proceed to represent the

G 3

impenetrable darkness of the cave behind
the figure, and instantly find that you
have a deficiency of power to give that
appearance of depth and recession which
you see in nature. You apply, at last,
your positive black; but even this will
not do; for black, when spread on your
picture, receives the same quantity of
light as the other colours, and is, therefore, when compared with the reality of
positive darkness, almost a light colour.
Having done, however, all that the means
of art will allow, you will be led to carry
your performance into your drawing-
room or study, and you will find that all
the darks that have been applied, are become darker by the change of situation;
but you will find also that the light parts
appear less brilliant in a much greater
proportion. The result of these experi-

ments, will be a distinct conclusion in
your minds, that the means which painting furnishes for imitating nature, are exceedingly limited on the extremes of the
scale of power; that you can make nothing
in painting so light, nor any thing so
dark; and you will immediately reject
the dogma of some professors, who pre-
tend to maintain, that there is nothing
black in nature, while it is evident that
the blackest object in nature has distinguishable shadows which are still darker.

If more simple demonstration of this
deficiency in the means of painting, on
the side of dark, should be required, let
the dubitant take a piece of the blackest
paper, or cloth, which he can find, without gloss; let him present it to the light
of the sun, holding at the same time his
hand or finger to obstruct the light from

a part of it, and he will find that the painter wants as much more power than he possesses, as the difference between a black object in light, and its possible shadows.

You will also conclude, from these premises, that the process of painting, whatever it be, which furnishes the most extended scale of means on the sides of light and dark, is to be preferred for the purposes of painting, if the results, after their accomplishment, be equally permanent. I am extremely anxious to impress these points on the minds of my auditors; because they influence the rules and principles by which colours are to be imitated as well as light and shadow, and upon which some of the great difficulties in art are ameliorated. But, in these examinations, you will perceive immediately,

that I have not taken into account the
splendour of light transmitted to the eye
in the exact angle of reflection from polished surfaces, or the radiance of self-
luminous bodies.   To represent the first
of these, the art is inadequate; and its
attempts to express the latter must be
attended with inevitable failure.   There
is, however, a picture by Claude Lorraine,
in one of the finest collections of this
country, in which the morning sun is introduced, and, together with the surrounding sky, painted with such rare
ability, that, if the rest of the subject
could have been executed with as much
truth, the picture would have been almost an illusion; but should the most
remote objects in it have been represented
as much darker than the sky as the reality
would appear, and had the same scale of

increasing dark been pursued by the artist,
he would have been obliged to have recourse to positive black in the middle
parts of his scene, without leaving himself
power to discriminate the nearer objects.
Again, pursuing the same reasoning further, what shall we say to those daring
painters who venture to attempt the representation of celestial appearances and
of poetical beings?   Shall we commend
and encourage their boldness ? They will
tell us, in the usual strain, that it is the
province of genius to aim at such representations, to take aerial flights, and to
reach "beyond the confines of this world;"
but common sense, duly comparing the
means which art or human intellect can
furnish for such enterprises, sees in the
visionary no other than a lunatic, who
dreams and fancies himself high in other

regions, till the chain which fixes him to his narrow cell, reminds him that he is destined to be an inhabitant of earth. Many painters, either misled or impelled, have attempted to paint, for instance, the transfiguration of our blessed Saviour; though the Evangelist says, " his face did shine as the sun, and his raiment was white as the light;" and others have shown a fondness for representing angels, although those agents of the Deity are always described as clothed with shining apparel, and as having a proportion of inherent brightness; but the most successful instances of this kind have exhibited nothing more than beautiful men, or children, or beautiful women, because the human mind has received no higher impressions which can be again communicated through the same organs.

Your education, in elegant reading, will have familiarized you to " the purple light of love," to " the rosy-fingered morn," to " the rosy-bosomed hours unbarring the gates of light ;" and these are all beautiful in poetry, the nature of which is to illustrate by proposing one thing for another to which it is something like. In painting, however, it is totally different ; and I would intreat you, for the proof of this principle, to endeavour to realise in your minds the last image to which I have referred, and then consider what a picture it would be. " The rosy-bosomed hours" will be a number of beautiful damsels, as beautiful as you please, taking a bar or bolt off a huge pair of gates. They have, however, red fingers, according to one poet, and scarlet bosoms, according to another. I appeal to your deliberate judgments, whether a picture so painted can be pleasing or useful ?   It cannot convey to the mind the dawn of a fine morning, nor can it gratify as a representation of a company of lovely maidens. The facetious Dr. Walcot, having viewed a picture of this subject in one of our national exhibitions, has humourously called it, in his Poems for Painters, " the brandy-faced hours." All this, however, does not go to preclude the representations, in picture, of Jupiters, Junos, Venuses, or any other of the Saturnian family of heathen deities ; because, if they were not really men and women, as it is most probable they really were, the poets, whose texts would be taken on these occasions, have represented them as such mere mortals, with all the vices, and with so few of the virtues of human nature, that the painter is at full liberty to make them subjects for his pencil.

These suggestions may be carried much further, with evident advantage, and always be productive of the same conclusions; you will, however, I am well aware, do this for yourselves, and probably do it much better than I could. I shall therefore proceed to state to you, some of the schemes and contrivances to which painters have resorted, for the purpose of evading the inevitable deficiency in the means of art, and in order to carry it further than it was ever likely to be carried.

The first of these is, to sacrifice or omit almost all the parts of objects that are rendered evident in nature by reflected light, thus throwing every mass of shadow

into a flat tint, and leaving the characters
of.the objects to be expressed by the pencilling that is bestowed on their surfaces,
supposed, actually in light. This scheme
proceeds on the principle, which is true
in itself, that a single colour, spread
smooth over an extended surface, may be
made darker, and yet retain an appearance of colour, than if it were subdivided
into parts. The first instances of this
kind are, I believe, to be found in the
works, the slight works, of our country-
man Wilson, so admirable in his best
performances ; and, subsequently, this
practice was established, as an indispensable rule of proceeding, by the late Mr.
Wright, known by his residence at Derby.
His example, however, has been exten-
sively followed ; because it abridges study,
it economises labour; and sometimes gives

an appearance of grandeur to the subject
which does not belong to it. We have a
landscape artist, who has brought this kind
of proceeding to a process so regular and
certain, that he will undertake to produce, from his individual pencil, a fresh
landscape every quarter of an hour, for
twelve or more hours successively. The
next scheme of this kind, and which is
generally employed for the purpose of
giving brilliancy and clearness to the skies
in landscape, is by making every thing in
the scenery, whether stationary or adven-
titious, darker than any part of the sky.
There is a splendid example of this kind
now in England, in the celebrated picture
by Claude Lorraine, which is nominally
distinguished by the appellation of the
Altieri palace, from which it was brought.
With the exception of the one deviation

from truth, which is frequent with the master who executed it, this picture is one of the most wonderful productions in landscape representation which the art of painting has ever achieved. Another mode of obviating the limited nature of the means of art, turns to the side of light, and is applicable principally to figure and other objects, usually contemplated near the eye. It consists in putting on the paint so thick, and in such quantity, that it may project considerably from the other surface of the picture; and thus, by receiving the rays of light in a more direct angle than the general plane of the performance, give an appearance of shine and glitter. Rembrandt, if I am not mistaken, was the first who resorted to this expedient, which has been so much followed by painters in oil-colours; but the pre-

H

sent state of his works, which we have in
England, would lead some, and has led,
to a belief that he relied more on this
contrivance than it is probable he did. It
is a practice with our cleaners of old pictures, to begin by cleaning off the old
varnish, in doing which they have also
cleaned off the thin glazing which covered
the projecting roughnesses in many parts
of the works of this master, and seeing
that it made the pictures glitter, whether
right or wrong, they have left them to
remain so. But, supposing a painter to
have gained something by this projection
of his colour for the representation of the
shine on metallic surfaces, it is probable
that the apparent gain will vanish when
the picture leaves his study : for it will be
placed in a different light from that in
which it was executed, and the lumps of

colour, thus throwing a contrary shadow, will defeat every intention of the painter. Besides this disadvantage, as pictures so painted grow in years, dust incorporates with the varnish, which always lodges round the interruptions to the unity of surface, and establishes a black rim to every one of them. Rejecting, then, all these expedients and subterfuges, we come to the proper definition of painting, the art of representing by means of colours, the appearances of natural objects and natural effects on an uniform plain surface.

The practices of drawing are not liable to these considerations, or, at least, not in the same degree. Drawing, which, as I have already stated, is properly but a preparative for painting, employs various means, in various modes, for the purpose

of indicating natural appearances as far as
the means and modes will allow. These
means would be confined to such few as
best answered the purpose intended by
drawing, if every one who draws was determined afterwards to paint; but as this
is not at present the case, and as many,
never meaning to go further in art, wish
yet for novelty in the practice, it may be
well to examine here, such modes of
drawing as are most deserving your notice.   The first is an expression of forms
only by simple lines, similar to the second
state of imitative art amongst the early
Greeks, and should be decidedly possessed
before any further advances can properly
be made.   This is the beginning common
to all the processes of drawing, and is of
very remote antiquity; for we learn from
ancient authorities, that the early Baby-

lonians had a practice of tracing out various figures, with a stylus or point, on
their bricks, while in a soft state, which
traces were afterwards filled with a red
colour, and gave a striking appearance to
their buildings. This appearance on the
walls of Babylon is mentioned in the sacred writings. The next degree of drawing is that which employs successive lines
to represent the shadows that express the
undulations of surfaces inclosed by the
outline. This, as a mode of study, is perhaps the best of all modes in the art. It
may be performed with a pen, but is
more frequently executed with black
chalk ; and when this material is applied
upon coloured or stained paper, the
brightest parts of the objects are also
touched with white chalk, making the
colour of the paper serve as a half tint,

The only objection that can be · urged against the use of chalks, in drawing, is their liability to be removed by even slight friction. A pleasant method, however, may be substituted for chalk-drawing, which is completely permanent. It consists in giving the effect of the subject very strongly with Indian ink, on white paper, and then tinting the whole with some even colour ; after which, the lightest parts may be scraped with a sharp knife, to show, more or less, the whiteness of the paper, and the effect of chalks will be obtained, without their inconvenience.

To water-colour sketches performed entirely in seppia, or bistre, or any brown colour, the most decided opposition should be made by every person friendly to the progress of art. In nature, the splendour of rich colour is to be found

only in the effulgence of light, which is
the cause of it; and this is invariably
diminished to the eye, in distant objects,
by the intervention of atmosphere, and in
shadows by the absence of light; yet in
the proceeding to which I object, the
shadows of the fore-ground, the middle-
ground, the distance, and even the shadows of the sky, are given with glowing
browns, while the light parts are left in
all the chilling purity of virgin snow.
This practice has such a tendency to
vitiate the eye, and to mislead the mind,
that there is great difficulty in correcting
its influence when once established. The
utmost stretch that reason will allow towards such practices is, in making the
foreground with brown, the middle with
a neutral colour, and the distance and
sky with grey. But to those who aim

H 4

not to acquire that use of colours, by which the fascinating appearances of nature are to be indicated, and sometimes even represented, I would recommend to confine their practices to the use of Indian ink, the most practicable and most delicate material which the painter in water-colours has yet been able to acquire; and for carrying this to a high degree of imitative excellence, I shall be able to furnish real philosophical grounds in a subsequent discourse.

There is another method of drawing, of a fanciful nature, which I mention only because it was occasionally exercised by the late ingenious Mr. Cipriani. The practice is, to roll up pieces of writing-paper, very tight and close, and then, having set them on fire in a candle, to extinguish their flame in the melted tallow, by which the points will give a brown, or even a black line, according to the degree to which the paper has been burnt. Of tinted drawing, I have already spoken, it is a most delightful process, and I shall have the honour of explaining it fully in another Lecture, when I mean to recommend it to your serious attention. It will not be expected that, in such an audience as this, I should give the time to say any thing on the subject of drawing, with a red-hot poker; because it cannot be regarded as other than a mere-frolic, somewhat inferior to copying pictures in wool or worsted.

There is, when figures are in question, an elegant manner of uniting miniature-painting with drawing, especially for the purposes of portraiture. The first examples of this kind came from the tasteful pencil of Mr. Cosway, now no more; but it may be carried, with advantage, somewhat further than his specimens, and I strongly recommend it you, because it may very soon be acquired.

I have no doubt, that if I were now addressing an assembly of those persons who attribute every thing good in the arts, to what is called genius, who expect, for themselves, to arrive at sudden excellence by a supposed inherent aptitude, I should be accused, on this occasion, of endeavouring to lower the dignity of painting, by confining its limits to visible objects. But to you, I am convinced, it will appear that I merely endeavour to show, that the practices of painting, to be good, must be founded in common sense; that they must be addressed to the reasoning powers of the mind; and that

they can never be carried higher than to
represent truly the highest possible degree
of visible created beauty, always in form,
sometimes, nay, frequently in colour, but
never in the full vigour of light and shadow. When this, however, shall have
been fairly and completely accomplished
by any one; we may, without hesitation,
permit him to go as much further as he
can ; but I am convinced, that whenever
a circumstance, so much for the real interests of the art, shall take place, the
successful operator will rest highly satisfied with his labours; nor complain that
his objects have been circumscribed and
easy.

I would, on this occasion, wish to recal
to your memories, a picture of Village
Politicians, which appeared a few years
since in the Exhibition of the Royal

Academy. The subject was so chosen as
to include nothing beyond the fair means
of painting, and it was so admirably executed, as to have continued for some
weeks the principal object of attraction
and conversation, to almost all classes of
this great metropolis. It will be highly
encouraging, further to remark to those
who are now setting out in the art, that
the picture, so justly celebrated, was the
production of a very young man. The
same judicious choice of subject produced
the same happy result, though of a much
higher kind, in that incomparable picture, The School of Athens, by Raphael.
It exhibits the most exquisite powers of
composition, of expression, and of fine
drawing, and yet there is not an object
introduced, in so comprehensive an arrangement, but what might be executed

faithfully, by such means as were in the artist's possession.

I have now to describe the different processes of painting, and their comparative advantages.

Painting in distemper was, unquestionably, the first process adopted, and probably consisted, in the outset, of nothing more than a rude application of the various earths, which chance might have discovered to the antediluvians; for we *will* suppose them to have had various kinds of earth, though the ingenious Dr. Burnet, in his Theory, has made the antediluvian world a beautiful, smooth sphere, entirely covered with fine rich pasture land. After a few experiments in the rude way just stated, it would soon be discovered, that the colours, so applied, might easily be rubbed or washed away, and this would lead soon to the use of some kind of gum, or gluten, by way of size, to prevent that inconvenience.

This was the state of painting in the early times of the Greeks, as I had the honour to show you in my first Lecture; the forms of figures being drawn, and the whole space coloured with some kind of earth, probably red.

No very great progress, however, could be made in the art, without discovering that tints were wanting, which the bosom of the earth could not supply, and the vegetable kingdom would probably then be resorted to; but the thinness of the juice obtained from plants and flowers, would ill suit with the ponderous nature of earths, and would, I think, immediately suggest the idea of throwing the tint on some kind of calx, for the purpose of giving it substance, as we find to be the case with some colours used at present.

Many improvements in the process were, doubtless, made by various practitioners amongst the ancients; but, as it was certainly practised, to its greatest perfection, in the beginning of the sixteenth century, at which period, also, it began to be disused, we will take Vasari's account of it, who was a celebrated painter of that time, in all the processes then known. " The Greeks, and after them the moderns," says Vasari, " used to glue a fine linen over the substance on which they meant to paint, lest it should crack or open at the joinings, and on this surface they spread a ground of whiting mixed with yolk of egg. The vehicle they employed for their colours, was a mixture of yolk of egg, with the milky juice expressed from the young stalks of the fig-tree, except in the case of blue, or of colours inclining to blue, on which occasion, the vehicle employed, was no other than common glue. In this process, every colour may be used that is proper for any mode of painting. The strongest size was always used in the last coating of colours." These pictures, I am persuaded, were afterwards constantly varnished; for we are told, that Apelles covered all his pictures with a darkish-coloured fluid to preserve them. We know that John Van Eych made many experiments, to ascertain the best varnish for such purpose; and we have a record in the reign of our king Henry III. which speaks of varnish, as at that time used for pictures, though it is known that they

were painted in distemper. All the scenery and decorations in our theatres, except those that are to admit the light
through them, are painted in distemper,
but with no other size than a weak solution of common glue. There are some
very serious disadvantages inseparable
from this process of painting. In the
first place, the colours become stiff and
impracticable soon after they are applied;
in the next place, all transparent colours
must be excluded, by which one chief
source of beauty is lost; and, lastly, as
all the light colours are to be made so
with *whitening*, which becomes darker by
moisture, every tint dries at least a hundred degrees lighter than it appears when
wet. On this account, the result is entirely a matter of calculation, and very
much a matter of chance.

I

Painting in fresco, has been long disused, on account of its extreme difficulty;
yet, when well executed, it exhibits the
greatness of a master more than any
other process, because every part must
be finished in the day in which it is begun, without the possibility of repairing
or retouching it afterwards.

It is performed on a ground of plaster,
spread over a wall, or other surface, of
which plaster the artist puts on only so
much as he can paint over while it will
naturally remain in a humid state; for if
any artificial means be used to protract
the drying, the masses of colour become
spotted and imperfect when dry.

With regard to materials, too, the painter in fresco is exceedingly limited, as he
can use no pigment that will not bear the
action of lime.   With these disadvan-

tages, with these restrictions to encounter, we must admire and wonder at the works which have, notwithstanding, been exe-cuted by the great masters of the Italian schools, in this process of painting; and if it require such promptitude, such high qualities to practise it, we cannot wonder that, in *these times*, it is entirely laid aside. Painting in fresco, has also the same ob-jectionable properties as painting in dis-temper, that the colours all appear opaque, and that they dry with an extreme differ-ence from their apparent tone, when first applied.

It will be easy, then, to conceive the extreme joy which filled the minds of the awkward, the ignorant, and the indolent, on the promulgation of *painting in oil;* a process that leaves the colours in a prac-ticable state for hours, and that will allow the making of one alteration or correction over another, until the loaded canvass grow under the hand of the artist into an actual, not an apparent, projection.

The discovery of mixing oils with the colours for painting, marks a distinct era in the history of the art. It was invented by John Van Eych of Bruges; but the secret of his practice did not travel into Italy till the time of Antonello da Messina, who spent many years in Flanders to study it. Returning to his native country, he stopped at Venice, where hé communicated his knowledge to Domenico Venizeano, who carried it to Florence, whence it spread to every part of Europe. It was soon found that colours, when mixed with oil, have a tender softness, which had not been seen in any picture produced before that discovery;

and the circumstance of the colours, so prepared, drying with less variation from their appearance when wet, than that which takes place either in distemper or fresco, became the cause that painting in oil was soon universally adopted. It was the custom of the first practitioners in this process, to cover the pannels of their pictures with grounds of thin plaster, which were then prepared for the colours by passing over them, four or five times, a sponge dipped in weak glue. The subject was then traced out accurately, and the colours, mixed up for use in fine linseed or sweet oil, though the latter was preferred, were applied with precision to the respective objects, the artist always working from the lightest tones to the darkest, and his white ground always supporting the brilliancy of his lights, because

always thinly painted. The fortunate
result of this mode of proceeding is now
obvious; for the oil pictures of Raphael,
of Leonardo da Vinci, of John de Ma-
beuge, and others, who painted thinly
over a white ground, remain, to this day,
with very small variation of their original
colour; while many pictures of the Venetian and other schools, which were
painted on red, or other grounds prepared
by oil colours, have sunk into their
foundation, and so far partake of the
gloomy colour, that the original subject,
in some, is scarcely discernible. After
the first period of oil painting, the mode
of practice changed considerably. The
first painting, or dead colouring of a picture, was now to represent the middle
tones of the subject; after which the
darks were added, and then the extreme

lights; but, as all on this principle were painted on dark-coloured grounds, the consequence has been destruction to the picture. This may be seen particularly in many of the pictures of Guercino, who frequently left the deep red, or black ground of the canvass, for the shadows of his objects.

Rubens attempted to revive the practice of the early Italian oil-painters, by executing all his pictures on white grounds; and they remain, at this day, more brilliant than the works of all his contemporaries who adopted a different system.

The inference from these remarks will be, that a white ground is of great importance in painting, and I wish to bespeak a place in your memories for this principle, as it connects with our subsequent enquiries. In the course of a few years, the first practitioners and admirers of painting in oils, discovered that they had cast off an old and faithful wife for some few defects in her nature, and had taken, without consideration, a beautiful and attractive mistress, who proved at last not to possess so many charms as had been attributed to her.

It appeared that though the colours in the processes of distemper and fresco changed materially as they dried, that colours, mixed in oils, became darker after they were-dry, and not only became darker, but turned to a yellowish colour, inimical to every taint that had a tendency to blue. Hence arose the custom amongst painters of mixing varnish and turpentine with their oils, to dilute and correct the first vehicle; but the inconvenience has not been removed by it.

Painting in water-colours, as now practised, had its origin with Mr. Sandby, as
I have stated already; and, so far as his
principle has been pursued, is founded in
the soundest deductions of reason and
philosophy.   As the practice of painting
in oils, from its superior advantages, su-
perseded the other processes then in use,
which were all in water-colours, so, I
trust, the practice of painting in water-
colours, as now understood, will, in time,
make good its unrivalled pretensions, and
become, finally, the current process of the
painter's art. My opinion, on this subject,
may surprise many who have not considered the subject before; but I would remind them, that if it be right to persevere
in processes of art, merely because they
have been practised for centuries, we
should be bound to condemn the first

patrons of painting in oils, which was then a novelty; and I would solicit nothing further for painting in water-colours than can be proved by sound reasoning, and chemical or philosophical experiment.

I have proved to you, I conceive, already, the importance of painting on a white ground, and the present mode of painting in water-colours cannot be exercised on any other. You will allow me, now, to lead you into a comparison of the two processes now chiefly employed by painters, premising that the principles by which I shall measure the respective powers of the two processes, considered as means of imitation, will apply equally to those of fresco and distemper; and I doubt not the result will be, that painting in water-colours will establish superior claims over the other three. I therefore beg leave to state, that, as the powers of painting are evidently limited both ways, that is the best process which has the most extensive scale; and this is to be found, unquestionably, in the practice of transparent water-colours upon white paper. The pure surface of a fine paper, which we leave for our highest lights, is as white as the whitest paint, before being prepared for use, and may be secured from all possibility of changing colour, by a vehicle perfectly without tint of any kind; but in painting with *oils*, the purest vehicles that can be used degrade the white so much that a newly-painted picture, in that mode, has the highest lights at least six distinct degrees less white than the white of paper. Here, too, I take no account of

the inevitable tendency of all light colours
mixed with oil, to become continually
darker, visibly darker, even in a few weeks,
and most decidedly so in a course of years.
Of this last, we have striking examples
in the works of Titian, of whom Vasari,
the contemporary of Titian, tells us that
it was then remarked, that the colouring
of his fairest females was of a chalky
whiteness; and hence, I think, I may
take the liberty of suggesting for your
consideration, whether this·be not the
cause, especially in highly-finished and
smoothly-painted pictures, why the best
copies, after the old masters, fall so far
short of their originals. The copy takes
up the original where it finds it, with the
light colours considerably degraded in
tone, and, having itself the same degradation subsequently to undergo, becomes

so much lower in the scale. On the side of dark, in the scale of means, we have exactly the same power as in oil; because there is no colour practicable in the one process that cannot be used with the same facility in the other. From these remarks, it should appear that our means for imitating nature, are more ample than those of the rival branch: but to this must be added, the natural result of painting on a pure white ground, by which every colour may be preserved with great, even with dazzling brightness, while, on the other hand, we have the power to make our tints as broken and subdued as our contemporary rivals.

It will, I dare say, be objected, that paintings in water-colours, are, and must be, very confined in point of size; that they are more liable to injury, and less permanent, than pictures in oil. It is of importance to answer these objections. The largest paper at present manufactured, does not much exceed four feet and a half, (no mean space for an artist to show his talents in,) and it *may* be made double that size; but there is a method, which I shall explain to you hereafter, of uniting the edges of two papers so closely in the same plane as to be imperceptible at a short distance. Therefore, by attaching the papers to pannel, or to canvas properly prepared, the size of our pictures may be extended to any given dimensions. As to the chance of injury, the pannel or prepared canvas defends the backs of our pictures, and the faces may be secured by a covering of fine isinglass, prepared in spirit of wine, which no ordinary moisture will again dissolve or penetrate. This covering, at the same time, gives transparency and depth to the shadows, vivifies the most brilliant colours, and yet leaves the highest lights as pure and untinted as before the application.

I now come to the important question of permanency: and, first, I may fairly state, that the tendency in all oils to turn yellow, in a greater or less degree, is never denied. The result of this, in the course of time, is, that the fleshy tints of the pictures painted in oil become brown and leathery, the white appears reduced to a dingy smoke colour, the greens to a disagreeable olive, and the blues to a positive green. The acute judgments of the most eminent Dutch painters, led them to reject, as far as possible, the use of positive blue, because

they were fully aware of the consequences;
and, on all occasions, they employed such
broken colours as would least injure the
general harmony, after the certain change
which they looked for should have taken
place. For the same reason, no doubt,
they allowed such an excessive brownness
in their shadows, as to make them sometimes perfectly foxy, a deviation from the
truth of nature which nothing but the
wish to correct an unavoidable defect in
their process could have induced them to
admit. Thus, then, the painter in oils
has nothing to boast for the permanence
of his colours. But it is often asserted,
in the language of untutored connoisseurs,
that the hand of time gives a mellowing
tint, which greatly improves a picture;
and, I cannot deny, that if the picture be
a bad one, ill-contrived, and discordant

in the tones and colours, it may be so improved; for the darker and less discernible it is the better. Yet if a painter have skill enough to make his performance what it ought to be, before it leave his easel, every change it can subsequently experience must be for the worse. Hence the man of taste, who expends large sums for the encouragement of this sort of painting, must either calculate on not living to see the objects of his purchase arrived at a state of mellowness and dingy perfection, or, seeing them perfect at first, he can entertain but little hope of bequeathing the same enjoyment to his successors. The unsophisticated admirer of nature and of genuine art, when he sees the bright azure of a noonday sky turned green, or the fair skin of a lady's arm turned to the colour of a wash-leather

K

glove, will feel nothing of gratitude to the hoary-headed father, Time, for these his boasted achievements.

To counteract, in some degree, these effects, I am persuaded that Titian, and some others of the Venetian school, painted frequently, if not always, their skies and distances in distemper colours; and then having varnished the whole with a very strong size, as they had be-fore been used to do, executed the re-mainder of their pictures in oil.* On the other hand, what can be objected to pic-tures painted in transparent water-colours, on paper, as being likely to prevent their permanency? The colours employed in them are all the same as those employed in the other process, therefore, of them-

* This opinion was entertained by Sir Joshua Reynolds.

selves; not more liable to change : besides,
the vehicles employed for preparing and
for using them, are entirely colourless,
and without any property that can operate
a change even in the most delicate tints.
It is true, that such of the reds as are
manufactured from cochineal, will become
somewhat paler, which they will do also
in oils ; and this is, therefore, no more an
objection to the one manner than to the
other. To those who feel an attachment,
a veneration, for the indistinctness, the
gloom that time throws over the labours
of the painter in oils, (which is the mis-
fortune, not the merit of his process), to
such the use of water-colours will afford
a means of imitation extremely simple,
and yet more certain to the copier than
can be furnished even by the same process, in which the original was executed.

This mode of proceeding will be described
to you in my next Lecture.

There are, further, in the mode of
painting I have now advocated, some
other advantages, highly important, and
that render it peculiarly suitable to such
as are students of the art from motives of
amusement only. In the practice of oil-
painting, the apparatus is cumbersome,
the preparation, which must be repeated
every time of sitting down to paint, dirty
and tedious ; and the effluvium proceeding
from the colours, if continued long, is
extremely injurious to the practitioner's
health. But in water-colours, as there is
no necessity for loading the intended picture with pounds of paint, the materials
and implements occupy but a small compass : they are ready in a few moments
for the most active and extensive exertions ; they can be taken up for any

length of time, however short, and quitted
at pleasure, and there is no circumstance
connected with them that can in the least
degree prejudice the most delicate consti-
tution.

It may, perhaps, be expected that I
should take some notice of painting in
crayons, as being a mode of proceeding
greatly admired by many, and being one
to which all those objections do not attach
to which pictures in oil are liable. Many
of those, however, which may be urged
against painting in distemper, may also
be urged against this mode, though it unquestionably possesses some beauties, in
the softness of appearance which it gives
to the most delicate flesh, and in the distant effects of atmosphere. But these
beauties, unless protected with the utmost
care, are transient and fleeting as the

flower of the field. The access of the external air, through even the smallest crevice, destroys many of the tints, the sun discharges others almost in a few hours, and the slightest touch is often ruinous to the whole. Recourse must therefore be had to a covering of glass, which, for a work of any considerable size, will be attended with enormous expense, and will likewise have the unfortunate effect of dazzling the spectator, as well as of altering the tints; for colourless glass, fit for protecting a large picture, has never yet been fabricated. To this may be added the chance that any accidental violence, destroying the glass, would most probably occasion the destruction of the performances also. Those, therefore, who look beyond the mere amusement of the moment; those, whose object is to hand down the thoughts, the features, and the

actions of men, to their distant posterity,
will scarcely be induced to bestow their
time on this fleeting branch of art, which
puts forth its bloom with the dawn of the
morning, and is withered and lost before
the decline of the evening sun.

I have devoted the whole of this discourse to the discussion of these points,
because I consider them as of the highest
importance ; first, as nothing is more necessary in every pursuit than to know
exactly the object to which we would proceed ; and next, as it is highly conducive
to our success to have a just consciousness
of the extent and value of our means.

When I have next the honour of addressing you, it will be for the purpose of
laying before you a method of proceeding,
founded in philosophical reasoning, con-
firmed by long experience, and such as

will make the practice of painting, to a
considerable degree of excellence, not difficult of acquirement. I flatter myself,
therefore, that I shall be able to convert
most of my present auditors into artists,
in some branch or other, and that, in
doing so, I shall have contributed materially to the stock of individual happiness.
To those who are of sedentary habits, the
cultivation of this art offers the most
liberal rewards ; for, in reading, the most
rational of all amusements, the mind is so
constantly kept in a state of abstraction,
as to benumb its faculties by a long continuance, unless in the perusal of books
merely entertaining, which have a tendency almost as bad. But a talent for
painting furnishes the most appropriate
and gratifying relief from books, by en-
abling the practitioner to embody those

ideas which he had before formed only
abstractedly in his mind, and thus to impress upon it, more forcibly, every kind of
knowledge. Besides, there are many objects of elegant accommodation, which
habit has made us require as part of our
comforts, objects that a talent of this kind
would enable us to embellish and aug-
ment. Those ladies, whose amiable manners and accomplishments have drawn
round them a circle of valuable friends,
will find the most heartfelt pleasure in
cultivating the practice of miniature painting, by which they will treasure up the
resemblance of each dear associate, and
thus hold sentimental converse with them,
even in absence. To such as travel for
the purpose of seeing distant countries, or
of examining our own, the practice of
drawing or of painting is of infinite ad-

vantage. Such persons are not deceived
by the apparent distance or magnitude of
objects under the ever-varying effects of
atmosphere. They understand the whole,
because they are accustomed to account
for such effects ; they see and enjoy many
beauties in nature, which escape common
observers, and contemplate, even with
·double pleasure, those that are obvious to
every one. But, above all, to such persons is this important consideration, that,
looking on travel as a means of instruction, this accomplishment conduces greatly
to that end; for the form will scarcely
ever be forgotten that has been once delineated, or that has ever been looked on
with a painter-like feeling.

And, let it not be supposed that I am
urging you to a pursuit attended with
great fatigue, or insuperable difficulty ; a

very high degree of excellence in drawing and painting, is certainly within every
one's reach.   Amongst the professors of
these arts, few are remarkable for very
close application ; and yet we see many
of them eminently successful while yet in
their youth.   The skill of many ladies and
gentlemen in painting, is also well known;
and we have a most encouraging instance
before us, in a gentleman of Exeter, who,
notwithstanding the fatigue of a very extensive practice in medicine, has sent up
to our annual exhibition some of the
best pictures of landscape that ever graced
its walls.

But there is another motive, that will,
I doubt not, have its due force in your
minds, to induce you to an assiduous study
of painting.   By that excellence, which
many of you, if not all, will certainly at-

tain in the course of a short time, you will stimulate the minds of our professional artists, blushing to be out-done by those, who have at the same time so many other pursuits; and thus you will have the further pleasure of contributing to the national stability, opulence, and grandeur.

But I trust you will not retire without carrying away in your minds, a complete conviction, that, in the discussion of this morning, and in the comparison that was necessarily connected with it, I have been uninfluenced by any personal consideration whatever. An ardent desire to establish the truth, and an unconquerable anxiety to serve the country at large, by promoting your improvement in this art, are my only motives. If I should appear to have employed in some parts of the enquiry, words of a stronger character than might have been advisable, I hope you will suspect my judgment, and not my intentions.

LECTURE III.

———

I HAVE stated to you, in my second Lecture, that the object of painting is to imitate nature, that has .existed, does exist, or might possibly .exist. I had the honour of reminding you, in the same morning, that the means for this purpose, are black and white pigments for the. extremes of power; together with blue, red, yellow, and their modifications and combinations. We will now, with your permission, proceed to examine some of the principles on which such materials are to be applied, so that a reasonable prospect of happy results may be entertained. I shall beg leave, therefore, to begin with offering definitions of the two terms, Tone and Colour, as they stand in relation to each other. The complete understanding of these terms, is essential to the particular discussion of this morning, as well as to the formation of a sound judgment in the art, either for practice or for criticism.

Tone, then, is the degree of dark that that any object has compared with white, independently of its kind of colour. Colour is that appearance, by which the extent of a surface is rendered distinguishable to the eye, as distinct from a surface of any other colour, independently of its tone. Thus it will appear, that two surfaces may be exactly similar in tone, yet of very different colours; or of the

same kind of colour, and yet very dis-
similar in tone. These definitions lead to
two others. Harmony of tone is that
gradual change from light to dark parts,
in which continued sameness and violent
contrasts are equally avoided. Harmony
of colours is that arrangement of them,
by which the contact of any two colours,
of a distinct and opposite kind, is prevented by an intermediate partaking of
both. From these explanations, it seems
to follow, that a picture may be discordant, at once, both in *tone* and in colours;
and that if a picture be harmonious in its
tones, such an advantage will prevent any
very violent disagreement of the colours,
however ill selected. Thus, then, we
shall properly give our first attention to
that part of the subject which furnishes
the most beneficial results in practice.

! There is, perhaps, no one part of the painter's profession that requires more sound science, or a greater proportion of mathematical knowledge in the arrangement of his compositions, than the proper distribution of light. This, however, fortunately for us, is deducible from axioms and admitted demonstrations; and the enlightened mind feels no embarrassment in their application. But the interference of what is called taste, to a half-formed artist or connoisseur, creates, sometimes, inextricable difficulties, by seeming, for it is only seeming, to set those rules and axioms at defiance. Taste will sometimes say, " This figure should be wholly in light;" when optical truth rejects the dictation. The same authority will sometimes say, " This or that leg or drapery in a picture should be in shade," when,

L

perhaps, it can be shown by mathematical demonstration, that the thing is impossible. The embryo connoisseur, just beginning to feel the principle, but not understanding it, pronounces, in such cases, with vague expression, yet with decisive manner, "This figure should be more prominent, that leg or that drapery should be more kept down." Hence, then, it appears, there is something to reconcile, according to the practice of many artists, between taste and mathematical correctness in distributing the lights and darks of a picture. I trust you will not think the time misemployed in an endeavour to conciliate these seemingly opposite powers, in the hope of effecting their complete union for the future. The consequence of this endeavour, I hope, will be to explode a notion now beginning to prevail, particularly amongst the painters in water colours, that a picture should be produced by feeling only, and not by reasoning. But what is taste? what is that mathematical censor which would control taste with so much severity? Taste is a prompt and delicate suscepti- bility, originally organic, or acquired by continual experience, to those appearances and demonstrations in nature and in art, which may be calculated to afford gratifi- cation to the senses. I can allow taste no higher employment. Judgment, the rigorous censor in such cases, where imi- tative art is concerned, employs itself in ascertaining whether the means that have been called into operation, for gratifying the requisitions of taste, are strictly con- formable to that adherence to truth which judgment imperiously demands. The rules and prescriptions of judgment, happily for mankind, are easily discover-ed ; the decisions of taste have not so obvious a foundation, though its leading principles may be traced and explained.

Variety is one of the chief sources of our pleasure in every pursuit, in every enjoyment. This principle, the proof of, which we derive from experience, and not from mathematical demonstration, pervades our commonest feelings. The sweet which we relish one day, would, if continued as our food for years, become no longer sweet; the acid that astringes our palates when we taste the lemon or the citron, would lose that quality to our taste, if we had no other nutriment. The good Creator of all things has shown that this principle makes part of his unalter-able laws in our favour. He has clothed;

it is true, the groves, the forests, and
the meadows with green, which he has
constituted the most wholesome colour
for our sight; but has he made that green
perpetual? Has he made any two objects of the same tint in this class? No:
he has distinguished each vegetable by an
appropriate tint, or by a polish of its
leaves, which therefore reflect a different
colour; he has, also, ordered these veg000et-
ables to change their colours in the rotation of seasons; but, with infinite wisdom
and goodness, he has ordained them to
change in succession; as, also in succession, when the spring dawns, they put
forth their various greens. Thus, then,
variety appears to be the first principle
which we can establish for examining the
prescriptions of taste for the diffusion of
light in a picture. If any one were to

set before us a canvass painted over with
black, we should look on it with indiffer-
ence; if it were replaced by one of white,
or of grey, we should still have no other
feeling. Again, if such a canvass were
equally divided into squares, or any other
figures of black and white, would it excite
a greater degree of interest in our minds?
Yet it is certain, that black and white,
with their intermediate modifications,
may be so arranged on a surface, that the
appearance, without any subject being
distinctly expressed, shall afford considerable pleasure to the eye. From this fact,
many rules have been formed by different
artists, of great eminence, for their successful practice, the most important of
which I shall endeavour to lay before
you. The first of these is, that there
should be in a picture three conspicuous

lights, differing from each other in size, form, and tone. The distances between these lights should also be as much varied. as possible, and their situation such as to place them in an irregular kind of triangle. It has been next prescribed, that the largest or principal of these lights should occupy about an eighth, or even a fourth part of the picture, and should, in general, be placed not far from the centre of the subject. In this principal light, the figure, figures, or other object which constitutes the chief interest of the composition, should invariably be placed. The figures, or other parts next in importance, as contributing to the primary object of the picture, should receive the second and third lights, amounting to another eighth part; and the mere accessaries, or subordinate parts should receive, by reflection

only, the degrees of light by which they
are rendered evident to the spectator.

In landscape pictures, the general practice has been to put this largest, or principal light, in the sky ; but an invariable
adherence to such a proceeding, would
tend to give the sameness of tiresome
repetition to the works of any master
who adopted it. But in cases, which will
sometimes occur, where the principal
figure or object is not of sufficient magnitude to occupy the whole extent of the
chief light, then, if the composition consist of moveable objects, the next in importance must be brought near, to form
a mass with the principal, and the other
lights must be thrown upon the most
considerable of the accessaries. It will
be important to know how far different
masters have conformed to these rules,
and in what degree their success has been

owing to such an observance of them. I
have had the honour of stating to you
before, that, from the time of Cimabue to
that of the great Raphael, the light and
shadow of pictures was very little studied.
Narrow shades were given along the lines
of the features, the folds of the draperies,
and the forms of the limbs ; and, invariably, where the painter supposed a mass
of dark to be wanting, he obtained his
end by the insertion of a dark-coloured
object. The pictures, therefore, of that
period, whatever they might be in point
of invention, composition, and drawing,
were, in their general appearance, flat, in-
sipid, and uninteresting. The first principle, with regard to tones, which seems
to have been perceived by the early Italian
painters, was, that a light is made brighter
by being opposed to a dark ; and, for
sometime, we find in their works a con-

stant association of some portion of dark
with every little bit of light, whatever be
its place in the picture. Giorgione was,
perhaps, the first who attempted to give
simplicity to his pictures, by the introduction of broad shadows and contracted
lights, and some of his portraits are, from
this circumstance, objects of the most gratifying contemplation. Titian, who imitated his fellow-student, Giorgione, caught
an idea of breadth from seeing his works,
though he appears not to have understood
the principle which produced them. The
pictures of Titian have, therefore, frequently great breadth of light and dark;
but it is often very abrupt, often scattered
at random, and generally produced rather
by dark colours than by proper shadows.
Correggio was, unquestionably, the first
painter who made the success of his works

to depend on the combination of light
and shadow ; and his most admired performances were fine examples of those
rules which I have just described to you.
But in viewing even those performances,
we must take these two cautionary remarks to assist us. The semitones, formed
by the reflected lights in his pictures, appear scarcely distinguishable ; and, by necessary consequence, the lights show like
so many insulated spots, for want of those
intermediates. This defect was certainly
not in those pictures in their original
state : it is an inevitable effect of the continual degradation of oil-colours, by which
the semitones, in pictures painted with
those materials, will be the first to disappear. With this caution, we must also
remember, that Correggio has occasionally made inaccuracies in regard to the

truth of his light and shadow, rather than suffer a dark part to divide what he had destined for his mass of light. This is an error in favour of taste, which a little more pains, taken with the composition, would have rendered unnecessary. In the works of Annibal Caracci, we sometimes find beautiful examples for the judicious combination of light and dark, though the same artist has also left us specimens, in which he has ruined his pictures, by introducing too little shadow. Both Nicolo and Gaspar Poussin are defective examples in this part of the painter's practice; and it is somewhat remarkable that, though they painted different kinds of subjects, the defect is in both of the same kind. Claude, commonly called of Lorraine, was by no means a master in the skilful arrangement

of tones : he adopted, however, the sim-
plest of all combinations, and very rarely
deviated from it. He made the near and
middle parts of his landscapes all dark,
the skies all light; and he connected and
harmonized these extremes by semitones
in the distance. I believe there is no
instance, at least I know of none, in
which he has tried a more complex arrangement and been successful in it. I
have no doubt this opinion will be deemed
a kind of heresy, or profanation, by those
enthusiastic admirers of Claude Lorraine,
who have given thousands of pounds to
purchase, sometimes even a single picture
by his hand ; but I appear before you to
assist your judgments, as far as may be in
my power, not to flatter prejudices, and,
therefore, I have no hesitation in adding
to my observations on this master, that

some of his finest works exhibit instances of inaccuracy, which one, who painted so deliberately as he did, could not have admitted had he known better. One of these inaccuracies I have had occasion to point out to you in my last lecture. Rembrandt is greatly admired by some for his combination of light and dark; because, by adopting a contracted light, and giving a much greater proportion of dark than of light, there results an unusual appearance of splendour on the spot that is illuminated. The blaze of brilliancy to be found sometimes in the works of this master, surrounded, as it always is, by an impenetrable obscurity, fixes attention immediately; and though it may justly be said, that this is a trick to obtain so desirable an end, yet it must be allowed, in favour of the great

artist who practised it, that, when once he
had fixed his choice on the effect of light
he meant to employ for his favourite purpose, he imitated its peculiarities most
truly.   In the portraits by Rembrandt,
we find the heads placed in a very strong
light against a black or very dark ground,
and that light rapidly dissolving into intense darkness as it proceeds down the
figure, till the whole picture exhibits but
one enlightened spot, which, in some
cases, is not more than the forehead and
part of the nose.   It is true, the solitary
appearance of such a light is now and
then relieved, and the monotonous darkness .cheered, by the introduction of a
hand in the lower part of the obscurity;
but this is not sufficient to do away the
characteristic of singularity by which you
are enabled to say at first sight, " This

picture is by Rembrandt." But his pictures now, amongst us have an appearance
of sparkle and glitter which I have already shown you they had not in their
original state; but which has misled
many of his modern admirers. It has
been esteemed and imitated by several
English artists within our own time. Sir
Joshua Reynolds, who constantly tried to
combine the vigorous light and shadow of
this master, with the splendid colouring of
Rubens, tried in his backgrounds generally to give this appearance of sparkling,
by spreading, on stumps of trees, grounds,
foliage, and even on skies, the half-dried
skins of paint from his nearly exhausted
palette, which he distributed about with
his palette-knife, or with his pencil-stick,
and then glazed them over with thin fluid
colours. Mr. Wright, of Derby, equally

deceived, endeavoured to imitate this unintended glitter of Rembrandt's pictures, by using a very coarse ticking to paint on, and then dragging his brush so lightly over the surface as to catch only the highest grains of it. We could pardon these mistakes in such great men, for who is perfect? and pass them over in silence, had the evil extended no further. But those circumstances, supported by such authorities, unfortunately became the foundation of a manner too prevalent in the British schools of painting and engraving not long ago. Every thing was then made to glitter with nobs of paint; and a contemporary poet, who lately wrote on landscape scenery, calls these, " Flickering flashes of celestial light." So much was this practice adopted, that the artist, far from seeing his mistake, em-

M

braced it more and more closely, and
sought for reasons to justify it. The
landscape painter might seem to gain his
justification in the effects of dews and
rains ; but the painter of figures obtained
the habit from a much more delusive
source. The casts after the antique statues, which he studied, and which, in the
original marbles, are characterised by a
beautiful gradation of shadows, are composed of a material which grows darker
by time, if light be excluded from it ;
and retains its original whiteness only
where it receives the light at right angles
to the direction of its surface. Hence
the lights on such casts are abrupt and
touchy, and hence the painter who studied them, and them only, imbibed a
mistaken notion, by which he was often
induced to make flesh, draperies, and

even skies, to appear as if they were
formed of polished metals.

I have very lately conversed with an
artist, the first now in this country, whose
early works, at the period to which I allude,
were characterised by this appearance of
splendid glitter, and there being, at the
moment, one of his works of that date and
class before us, he very candidly acknowledged that he considered such a practice as
having led to one of the most objectionable
properties of his juvenile performances.
The beautiful specimens which come now
from the same pencil, have nothing of this
kind in them, unless the objects naturally
require it, and then he is most eminently
successful in the imitation. If we look
to the great examples in painting which
the Italian schools have left us, we shall
discover nothing of this kind; and the

M 2

judicious eye, employed in this research, will prefer the sterling ore of the great master, to the tinsel of untutored pretenders. Even Rubens, the most splendid of all painters, was infinitely above the artifice of attempting to *shine* by representing his objects as if made of shining materials.

Returning, however, from examples to precepts, for the distribution and management of light, we have to learn that the semitones, or those degrees of light which are occasioned by reflection, should occupy about one half of the extent of the picture, and that the positive dark should cover nearly the remaining quarter. It certainly will not be understood by this, that a picture is to be formally divided into a half and two quarters, of which the first is to be given to the semitones, and the other

two to the extreme light and the intense
dark; but that the quantity of each of
those principles, if collected together,
should form so much of the surface of the
picture. It has also been prescribed, that
the light should never be carried close to
the outside of a picture, and, in general,
the rule is worthy of attentive observation; yet I have seen instances in which
the light on the foreground of a landscape
has been brought down to the base line
with the happiest effect. If such ground
be supposed to represent an eminence,
and great depth or distance of view required to be shown, this practice is almost
indispensable; but it requires all the skill
of a consummate artist to prevent the
effect being disagreeable. These are the
chief rules which taste has established for
the quantity, the arrangement, and the

M 3

modifications of light in pictures. They
are proved by experience to be founded
in the nature of our feelings, as affording
that portion of variety which is necessary
to pleasure. But, on the other hand,
truth, rigid, mathematical truth, demands,
that when the direction of light for the
subject of a picture is once chosen, and
the objects arranged, such and such certain parts or objects shall be in shadow.
Hence, then, proceeds the great practical
difficulty that a painter has to encounter,
and which makes his successful performances almost inestimable ; for he must be
able, by continual habits of careful study,
to arrange every part of his subject completely in his mind, before he make an
attempt to paint. He must do this, not
only with reference to the truth and contrast of forms, but also to the situation

and direction of those forms, compared
with the direction of the intended light,
that the enlightened mathematician may
be able to prove every degree of light to
be most correctly in its place, and yet
that the most accomplished and tasteful
connoisseur shall have cause truly to say,
that, in the arrangement of those lights,
his most sanguine wishes, with regard to
the feelings of taste, have been antici-
pated.   Thus, then, we are arrived at the
full object of our present inquiry.   For
we find that taste, in the distribution of
light, requires nothing incompatible with
truth ; and that mathematical correctness
will rather aid, than obstruct, the beautiful
combinations of light and dark.   It is true
we see many pictures, unexceptionable in
point of correctness, that excite no interest in the spectator ; but they are the

works of such as would sit down to make
pictures by rule and compass.   It is likewise true, that we see many pictures
which please at first sight, to a high degree, by their happily combined tones,
and afford us no gratification on reviewing
them ; because they are the productions
of such as work from feeling or taste only.
To make the result such as it ought to be,
both principles must unite in the operator.

To the painter, then, it appears, the diffusion of light and the harmony of tones,
is of high importance, in delighting that
organ by which he is to carry the sentiment of his composition to the spectator's
heart.

We will now transfer our attention
from the consideration of light in its simple state, to the consideration of colours,

which are the effects of its decomposition.
Colouring is divided, as it relates to painting, into two parts; first, as it is matter of
imitation, and again, as it is matter of
combination and arrangement. It is on
the latter of these principles that I mean
to take up the subject, first, in our enquiries of this morning. This subject, as
it relates to the spectator, is the most
sensual of all the qualities in a picture;
but, as it relates to the artist who practises
it, is a study of most extreme difficulty.
Here taste seems to sport almost without
control, and the painter, to ensure a successful combination, must have his eye
made accurately susceptible of small dif-
ferences and agreements, both by the
study of nature, and by the repeated investigation of *their* works who are allowed
to have excelled in this department, that

he may be able to understand and apply the principles which the dictates of taste may afford. It is true, however, that the same colour does not, owing to the various structure of the visual organ, afford the same pleasure to every eye; nay, it has even been ascertained that some persons, who distinguish and judge of forms with accuracy, do not perceive colours at all; and it is well known, that several of the members of a family now living, see green as if it were red. I mention these extreme cases, not because they frequently occur, but to show the probability of there being many lesser modifications of these peculiarities, which we can determine to exist only by their effects. Upon this supposition, I would account for the different manners of colouring which we see in the masters of various schools and countries ; some allowing a general tint of green to prevail in their works ; others, who are more numerous, admitting a general tint of brown into every picture, and some giving the preference to blue or lead colour. I can conceive many instances in which students in painting, misled by the reputation of celebrated masters, have adopted and persevered in their manner of colouring, though it probably originated in a natural defect; but we should always oppose to these instances, the truth of nature, in which there is no manner whatever; and we should remember that peculiarity, like a wayward child, becomes more unruly the more it is indulged. These remarks, however, are rather digressive.

Colours are blue, yellow, orange, red, purple, violet, and green. These are divided by the optician into primitive and compound ; and they are divided by the painter, into warm and cold.   The warm are the yellow, orange, and red, together with such compounds as incline decidedly to them ; the cold colours, are the violet, blue, and green, and such mixed colours as have blue for their principle.   But it will be evident, on a moment's consideration, that the three compound colours, as denominated optically, may be either warm or cold, as partaking most of the red or yellow on one side, or of the blue on the other.   The warm colours are understood to attract, and seemingly to approach the eye; the cold colours, on the other hand, are considered as having a tendency to give the appearance of receding.   This principle is probably true to a certain extent ; but it depends on another, which will be referred to hereafter, either to enforce or counteract it. To the seven colours, have long been attached emblematical significations; and painters, even from the infancy of the art, have adopted the association. It, therefore, becomes necessary to speak of the circumstance, as one that will enable us more forcibly to feel the sentiment of many pictures of the old masters. It is true that this, like all other kinds of emblematic representation, has no effect but on those who are previously acquainted with the means of interpreting it; yet it may furnish ideas to future practitioners. Yellow is understood to represent lustre and glory; red, to represent power and love; blue, implies divinity; purple, authority; violet, humility; and green, servitude. Upon this statement and explanation, we are enabled to account for the invariable practice amongst painters of pourtraying the blessed Saviour of mankind in garments of red and blue: the red implies his comprehensive love to the human race, as well as his power to fulfil the dictates of that love; and the blue signifies his divine origin.

But colours, as the means of painting, are required to be brought together for various representations, and it is necessary to consider what action they have on each other, by contrast or agreement; for it sometimes suits the painter to separate his objects by a difference of tone, or by a difference of colour, and sometimes to unite them by the concordance of one or both principles. The prismatic arrangement of colours, will give us the first rule to adopt for the placing of colours, where

2

the subject is left to the artist entirely: in that, the primitive colours are always harmonised by means of the intermediate compounds; as red and yellow, by orange; blue and yellow, by green; and red and blue, by purple or violet. But proceeding beyond this, we must take black and white into our list, as colours with the painter, though not with the optician. The extreme disagreements of colours are in placing the primitives near to, or upon each other, though this disagreement, where the association is unavoidable, may be, in some degree, abated, by making each of nearly the same tone. Colours may be contrasted, and even beautified, by placing them on other colours of a compound nature, in which one element is the same as the colour to be contrasted; and the contrast and the con-

sequent distinctness of the first colour will
be greater or less, in proportion as that element is admitted or rejected. From these
facts, we may deduce some practical rules.
White, which exists only by contrast,
suits well on any darkish-coloured ground,
and with any light one, except yellow
and blue, both of which lose a great part
of their brightness by the vicinity. Light-
yellow has much clearness and beauty on
purple and green; light-blue suits well
on green, violet, and yellow, not very
pale; light-green, inclining to yellow, has
a good effect on purple, violet, and blue;
but red upon red, purple upon red, or
blue upon a darker blue, should never be
allowed, unless there be the means of
contrasting the upper colour *so,* by some
opposite one in its neighbourhood, as to
restore the degree of colour it will seem

to have lost by being placed on a darker tint of its own kind. By means of these guides we will form a combination of co-lours for a picture, which will be a perfect example where we have the choice of our materials for composing it, and will very greatly assist us where we may chance to be limited. Let it be a group of figures, or a bunch of flowers, the combination will be equally proper and beautiful. We will take, first white, then yellow, then orange or pink, then scarlet, afterwards crimson, next purple, and then blue or green, arranging these from the central light, towards the outsides of the picture, or into the dark. But though these are to be the chief masses of colour, and such their arrangement, the subject must be so contrived, that near each colour there shall be introduced some small portion of

N

its opposite, that the value and true colour of each may be made evident, without enforcing it so as to injure the principle of harmony, which is, above all
considerations, to be studied. Thus near
the white must be introduced some small
part of dark, or its whiteness will not appear; near the orange or scarlet, some
parts that have a tendency to blue, grey,
or cool green; near the purple, somewhat
of a yellowish green; and near the blue,
something inclining to orange, tawny, or
red brown. All these arrangements must
be considered as subject to the rules
which have been discussed this morning,
for the government and distribution of
tones. It is not to be understood that I
am speaking of these several colours as
constantly pure and unmixed; but that
such situations in a picture should be oc-

cupied by such colours, or their modifications. If the subject admit of, or
require unbroken colours, then the rule is
specific ; if it require tints less pure, then
the rule applies generally, by breaking
the surrounding colours in the same proportion as the first or central colour is
broken. But there are many cases in
which, the subject being prescribed to the
artist, he is embarrassed by finding the
object, which must receive his chief light,
not of a colour to be made interesting to
the eye, without great art in the management. On such occasions, the colour of
the object must be distributed as much as
possible over the picture, in all its modifications, and contrasted and enforced
near the figure itself, by whatever colour
will give it most the appearance of that
which it seems to want. In subjects of

landscape, if the beautiful bloom of spring be required in the picture, the artist will find himself incumbered with the profusion of greens; yet, even in these, the varieties are almost innumerable to an attentive observer; and I know not why, unless for the difficulty, a season, · so blooming and full of interest, should be almost discarded by painters. The general hue of such pictures, when executed, will be of a cool kind, broken by the various colours of earths, and enlivened by the introduction of gay and youthful figures. In representations of autumnal landscape, the artist has all the varieties of broken colours at his disposal; and his combinations should, therefore, be of the most perfect kind in this class. It is, then, only in portrait representations, and in some subjects of still-life, that the professor of painting has to tremble for the success of his colouring, as a matter of combination. Yet, even in these, the principles we have examined and adopted this morning, will greatly assist to sur- mount the difficulty. The backgrounds, which make so considerable a part of portrait pictures in these times, afford great facilities in extending or concealing the forms, in distributing, contrasting, and harmonising the tones and colours. In the days of Holbein, the painting of a portrait consisted of nothing more than a faithful representation of the head, placed against a flat screen of some dark-coloured velvet, on which a damask pattern of large flowers was usually painted; but, in these days, when the practice of this branch of art is, in many respects, so greatly improved, we see ladies and gen-

tlemen blooming against scarlet curtains,
smiling with noon-day faces against evening or moonlight skies, and reclining in
luxuriant arbours of fragrant flowers.
With these additional materials to work
on, the portrait pictures of the present
British school should be, in point of combination, as they certainly are, superior to
any that have preceded them.

Colouring, as a matter of imitation, in-
volves many and extensive difficulties,
though none that may not certainly be
surmounted, because in this part of the
practice of painting, there is always a
visible standard to which the performance may be referred, in order to ascertain its degree of success or of failure.
But as the success of painters, in imitating the human complexion, has usually
been so far considered a test of general

skill, that it has given the appellation of a good or a bad colourist, we will take this branch only for our present observations. I shall propose to you first to go through the colouring of a head in a process of water colours, which comes nearer to the philosophical principles on which the appearances of nature are founded, than any other process of painting as yet known. You will begin by considering the object you mean to imitate, as if it were of a pure white material. You will then come to one very important conclusion in art, that positive shadow is black, and that any lesser degrees of it are modifications of black and white. You will proceed therefore to represent your object in the state of appearance which it has by its light and shadow. This being accomplished, your next proceeding will

N 4

be to insert the grey tints ; which are of
two classes, the local, and the accidental.
The first are those which arise from the
skin, showing the larger veins through
the thinness of its texture, and the latter
are those which appear from the edge of
the shaded surface of the solid flesh,
showing through a part of the enlightened surface of the skin, and which depend for their quantity on the direction
of the light and the situation of the
spectator with regard to the object
in view. The next proceeding will
be to insert the tints which tend
to red, which are all local, and generally composed of modifications of
crimson and scarlet. The complexion
colour will then be passed over all the
other tints and shadows, and will be
done in water colours, which I am
now particularly recommending, with a

mixture completely transparent, leaving
the highest or shining lights untouched; but in oil colours this will be performed with a semi-opaque mixture,
and the highest lights added upon it.
When brought to this state, your figure
requires the reflected colours to be inserted in the shadowed surfaces, and the
last finishing of the shadows, observing
always, in this part of the proceeding, to
encrease the redness of the dark touches
about the features, and in every other
part of the figure where the light, passing through the thin texture of the flesh,
takes and exhibits the colour of the medium it has passed through.   But it may
happen that the quantity of the greys
and reds which precede the general, or
complexion colour, have not been duly
given; in which case, the defect must be
corrected by careful additions, after the

general colour, and before the finishing. At this period, too, you have the figure in a proper state for giving to it the particular hues observable in the works of the most eminent colourists, except Rubens. If you wish to convey an idea of the manner of Guido or Carlo Dolce, you will finish with a violet tint; if of Rembrandt, with an olive green; if Titian, with burnt umber; if of Vandyke, with a purple brown. I have purposely excepted Rubens, because, though the most splendid of painters, the colouring of his complexions is an entire deviation from the truth of nature. For a fair person, he takes white, or pale yellow, for his brightest light; this is always succeeded by a bright rose colour; the rose colour by a distinct violet tint, and that by a foxy brown, glowing sometimes in

the shadows with decided scarlet.   If
Rubens have occasion to introduce the
swarthy, sun-burnt figure of a man, he
makes the highest light yellow, the general colour of a dark tawny, the edges
of the shadows of an olive green, and the
dark shadows approaching to a rich coffee
colour.   I allude only to these most distinguished masters on account of the
short time allowed for the discussion,
though there are many other painters of
considerable estimation, to whose works
similar observations may be applied.   It
will, however, be evident to you from
these remarks, that every one displays a
preference for some particular hue or
tint in his figures, which constitutes what
is called his manner of colouring.   I may
properly take this opportunity of recommending to such of you as wish to copy

the pictures of the old masters, either for
the purposes of study. or in order to preserve faithful duplicates of them, to do
it invariably in water colours. All colours mixed with oils of any kind, as I
have shown you already, have a tendency
to become very considerably darker by
time. The great works of foreign schools
which have been handed down to us, have
all undergone this degradation of colour,
and, if you copy them faithfully as they
now appear, in a process which will make
your work liable to the same change, the
similitude will be lost in a few weeks.
The process of painting in water colours,
such as it is now understood and practised, is the most permanent mode of
painting at present known, . and is the
only way we now possess of perpetuating
many valuable oil pictures which are ra-

pidly advancing to that state, in which their beauties will be entirely lost to us and to posterity.

Little more remains to be added, on the subject of colours, to the remarks I have made already, except to caution you against a very delusive advice given by Du Fresnoy, whose poem has, unfortunately, been held up as the guide to artists, and has been even more generally circulated than before, by the influence of Mr. Mason's very elegant translation, and of Sir Joshua Reynold's notes. He recommends, by way of producing harmony in the colouring, to make all the shadows in a picture of the same colour. In giving this advice, he proves that his observation of natural effects was extremely superficial. For it is true that the shadows in all objects do approximate to the same appearance by the absence of light. Light is the cause of every kind of colour; in the privation of light the surface of every object is black, and the modes of a coloured object in its shadows when it is partially enlightened, as we usually see objects, is just so much differing from the colour of its lights as the proportion of black which constitutes the degree of shadow added to the colour of the lights. Shadow, then, is one of the chief agents which nature employs in harmonizing her combinations; yet it is not to be imitated by making all the shadows in a picture of brown, blue, green, or purple. In the harmony of colours, therefore, as it is in the harmony and distribution of tones, there is much to be done, much to be understood by the artist, in order that taste and judgment may both be satisfied. If we mean to

practise the sublime art of painting, which
gives to the deliberate contemplation of
the chamber and the closet, every perfection of form which the Divinity has
allowed us to imagine, let us weigh, with
reverence and philosophical exactness,
the due measure and effects of that light,
by which objects are made to recede or
advance, by which forms are rendered intelligible to us. If we mean, merely, to
inform ourselves in this art as judges,
that, by our future decisions, the art itself may be promoted, and the interests
of the state essentially benefited, let us
feel that it is our duty to be correct in
those opinions which we mean to enforce upon others : let us seek, anxiously,
for truth, and endeavour to support it.

" Let there be light," was one of the
earliest commands imposed upon chaos,

and the painter who shall neglect to study, and shall fail in the skilful distribution of it in his works, will produce such pictures, that the judicious spectator, in looking on them, may truly be led to say, " Chaos is come again."

LECTURE IV.

THE objects that nature presents for the imitation of the pencil are infinitely various, and almost as much so in the different degrees of interest they excite. But the human figure, and the numerous combinations that may be formed from it, are, beyond all comparison, the most *important*, and will furnish ample matter for our discussion of to-day. It is by the human figure only, that the painter can excite passion, or convey sentiment. In subjects of still life, however judiciously chosen,

o

however finely executed, it is only the judgment of the spectator that is gratified, — the heart remains untouched; in the finest pictures of the finest landscapes in nature, if they appear untenanted by human beings, we shrink from the joyless waste, and cling to society. . With pictures of figures, whatever be their kind, we seem to hold a sort of intercourse, and, as they hang round our solitary apartments, we almost cease to feel ourselves alone. By representations of figures, the painter may inspire the most fervent indignation, the most thrilling horror, and he may warm the gazer's bosom with pity, admiration, or joy. It ought not, however, to be concealed, that, if the powers of this branch of art be much greater than every other, and its exercise as much more gratifying, the acquirement of it, though within every one's reach, is attended by an equal proportion of difficulty.

The first object of practice in this pursuit is to draw repeatedly the most perfect human forms, till the idea of each kind be so strongly impressed upon the mind, as to enable you to draw the same forms again correctly from recollection. But a great embarrassment will arise in the mind, as to the means of procuring such forms to study. To trace out, as every painter must do, the perfection of human beauty, through the various individuals who possess more or less of its constituent parts, would neither be compatible with your many other pursuits, nor with the delicacy of your feelings. Fortunately, however, the great masters of ancient sculpture have left us some incomparable examples in every species of beauty that has at any time been observed, or that ought to be looked for amongst men. Of these the copies, or casts, are very numerous in this country, and are consequently accessible to every one. In them you will find a variety of proportions both in the structure of person, and in the length or the solidity of the limbs; but all approaching the general standard of proportion which has, doubtless, been laid down to you by your drawing masters, or which may be found in almost every book that professes teaching to draw. I have endeavoured to show, in my second Lecture, by what means you may acquire an unerring consciousness and perception of visible beauty; and an intimate acquaintance with those works of Greek and Roman sculpture will greatly facilitate the acquisition.

There is a very extraordinary work by Rubens, on the character and beauty of the human figure, which work was in manuscript, in the late king of France's library, with drawings to illustrate its principles, made on the margin by Rubens's own hand. The leading idea of it is worthy the bright mind that conceived it, and consists in supposing, that, as man was created at first after the image of his Maker, he must have been *then* infinitely beautiful; but that as, after his fall, he became the prey and victim of his passions, his form and countenance gradually approached to a resemblance with those animals of the *brute creation* which are characterised by such passions as he pre-eminently indulged. The examples he gives, in various drawings, to prove this, are highly ingenious; and,

I think, the principle seems so far founded
in reason, that, if adopted with some re-
serve, it might tend greatly to assist you
in giving force to individual characters in
your historical compositions. This work
also contains another principle truly deserving your notice, in *stating* that the
elementary form in the figures of men, is
the square or cube; in females, the oval
or egg-shape; and in children, the circle
or globe. This, if rightly understood,
will lead you a great way in making up
your minds on the true forms of human
figures. The difficulty of becoming perfectly acquainted with each kind of figure,
I must advise you again, is not inconsiderable. I have stated to you, before,
how little chance there is of your meet-
ing, in any individual, all the various
parts necessary to constitute a perfect

example of that species of beauty, whatever it be; and the consequent *necessity
of going* through a long course of studies,
in order to acquire this indispensable
knowledge, would postpone the pleasur-
able part of your practice to a distant
period.   However, this great difficulty, at
first sight so discouraging, is obviated, as
I have said before, by the beautiful specimens remaining to us of ancient sculpture.   In them we find almost every
different kind of human beauty thoroughly
studied, and exquisitely displayed.   Whether some of them, reputed of Greek
origin, be so or not, is of little importance
on the present occasion.   Mengs, in his
most incomparable writings, expresses an
opinion that they are not; but they are
full of truth, grace, and beauty, and those
properties are the proper objects of your

attention. Several of them, of masculine
figures particularly, it is worthy of remark,
are chisseled in a manner to represent the
plaiting and the granulated surface of the
human skin. This circumstance appears
to have escaped the notice of those artists
and critics who assert, that the ancients
had little or nothing of minute imitation
in their figures. Those which seem to
me most calculated to engage your attention, are, The Piping Fawn, The Apollo
of Belvedere, The Venus di Medicis, The
Family of Niobe, a light and elegant figure
of Mercury, with his feet across, and
many busts of particular characters, of
which the casts are very common amongst
us. I would entreat you to add to these,
correct drawings from all the casts after
Frammingo, that may come in your way.
As representations of children (infants

most of them), they are so exquisitely true as to become almost illusive. .

Yet, in prescribing the sculpture of the ancient Greeks and Romans, as models for your imitation and study, I wish, most anxiously, to impress on your minds a caution that is indispensable. The performers of those excellent works, admired for so many ages, appear to have been fully aware of the great expression that arises, in nature, from the dark pupils of the eyes, and from the generally dark colour of the eyebrows ; but, unable to represent colour in their sculpture, on such occasions, they have adopted the dangerous artifice of sinking the eyes, and of raising the thin part of the nose nearly to a level with the forehead, by which they obtained, in almost every direction of light, dark shadows about the eyes, as substitutes for that colour which they could not express. This practice, and the motives of it, are so obvious, that I should not have taken up your time to notice it, were it not for the laborious anxiety which some persons, artists as well as others, have manifested to prove that this was really the construc- tion of the ancient Grecian face. We find nothing of this defect in those heads of antique workmanship which profess to be portraits ; and I dare venture to assure you, that such a face, with the forehead and the nose in straight line, never did exist in nature ; and I am persuaded that if one ever should exist, it would be uni- versally regarded as a deformity.

It is greatly to be wished, that we had as many examples of the paintings of the Greeks and Romans as we have of their sculpture. It has been inferred by many,

18

that because their statues are so tran-
scendent, their works with the pencil
must have been so too; but this reasoning appears to me founded in conjecture
only, and I dissent from the conclusion
for many reasons. The forms of the
figures in their pictures, may have been,
and doubtless were, finely imagined, and
correctly drawn ; for form, at that time,
appears to have been much studied, and
well understood. But much more than
this is requisite to make fine pictures.
Composition, light, and shadow, and colouring, are all indispensable, and *these*, I
very much incline to think, they possessed
in a very limited degree. The grouping
in those specimens of ancient painting
that have reached us, seems to have gone
no farther than arranging all the figures
in a row, nearly on the same base line,

sometimes almost without varying the distances between them; and their greatest efforts that I have seen, extend no further than sometimes bringing *two* figures together, placing *one* in a sitting or recumbent position. These are mostly on a perfectly black ground, and have no variation of distance supposed in the objects. The extravagant praise bestowed by some ancient writers on the best pictures of the Greeks, is not decisive in their favour. They certainly must have been greatly superior to the performances of the Egyptians, from whom they, doubtless, received the art; and as, therefore, they surpassed all that had gone before them, they received the highest praise that language could bestow. But the case is different in modern times : for we have none of the best specimens of the

Greeks remaining, and hence give them
full credit for the amount of their reputed
excellence, while, feeling that our own
works are defective, we judge them, consequently, inferior. It will, doubtless, be
urged, again and. again, that from the
exquisite skill with which sculptures were
executed in ancient times, we may fairly
infer that the practice of painting also
was excellent. But this is merely a pre-
sumption, and, I think, carries, as I have
said already, little weight with it. The
two arts are so distinct in their object and
their means, depending for their success
on causes so totally different, and requiring modes of education, in the respective
professors, so unconnected with each other,
that it is certainly possible for either art
to flourish in a high degree where the
other is but little practised. The super-

stition, the idolatry of the ancients, led,
necessarily, to the highest improvements
in sculpture, while the efforts of the pencil
seem to have been confined more to domestic purposes. If we look into the history of arts in our own country, we shall
sometimes find that of sculpture more advanced, sometimes that of painting most cultivated and improved, and always without
any appearance of a dependence on each
other. It is, true, some learned painters
in modern times have been at great pains
to fix upon the painters of ancient Greece
the credit of deep and philosophical reasons in preparing and executing their
pictures; but these essays prove, in my
mind, nothing more than the ingenuity
and classical reading of their authors;
and I should certainly be disposed to
arrange them with those profound com-

mentators on the beautiful verses of
Homer, who have extorted from many
passages of them, thoughts and allusions
that never entered the mind of the Ionian
bard. An instance to illustrate this
came some time since within my own
observation. An ingenious artist, who is
now no longer living, had read in Pliny,
or in some of the Greek writers, the description of a picture, painted by a great
master, of the battle of Marathon, in
which description, it is said, that the
figures were so exquisitely finished, that
they appeared to sweat with exertion.
The classical artist took this for matter
of fact, though certainly no more than
an ornamental expression; and actually
painted several pictures, in which he
rubbed the figures over with various kinds
of oils, in hopes to find some way of

rivalling this reported excellence in the ancient Greek painters. But though deprived of any assistance from the works of the ancient Greek painters, we yet possess most excellent examples performed nearer to our own time, in various parts of modern Europe. With these, and the casts or marbles which I have proposed for your consideration, you will soon be enabled to acquire a sufficient fund of painter-like knowledge, for the purpose of imitating the animated forms of nature. But you will then feel the necessity of arranging into classes the various combinations of which human figures are capable, and, perhaps, of applying to some one of them only, as inclination shall decide. To excel in all of them has been found too great a task for the greatest painter that has yet existed. The great division of subjects, composed of figures, is into the *sublime* and the beautiful. The first of these may be subdivided into the *terrific* and the *grand*; the last into the *elegant* and the *rural*, which will, I think, include every species. I shall endeavour to direct your judgments in the proper mode of treating each of these classes, in the order in which I have named them; but I beg permission first, to offer some remarks on the choice you should make of subjects in general : if I should appear to you to be mistaken, you will pardon me.

At a time like the present, when we ought to look beyond our own country only for the purpose of counting our enemies, the enemies of integrity and honour, it is right, it is necessary, to emblazon, by every means we are possessed of, the heroic virtues of our countrymen, to celebrate the happiness

and the domestic virtues that grow out of
British freedom. If we look for subjects
of sublimity, let us endeavour to pourtray
our native ancestors, thronging to defend
their shores from invading legions ; if we
look for subjects of grandeur and pathetic
interest, let us endeavour to represent our
great, our incomparable Alfred, breaking
his last loaf with the pilgrim that entreated
alms at the door of his retirement, or to
paint him triumphing, like a matchless
warrior, over the Danish ravagers of his
country ; if we wish for subjects of grace
and elegance, the various history of our
noble ladies will furnish ample materials in
all ages ; if we wish to depict the successful labours of the industrious peasant, or
the comforts of his peaceful home when at
rest, where shall we find the reality but in
Britain ? We will not, then, fly to Athens
or to Rome for subjects to embellish our

pictures, we will not seek in Arcadia for shepherds and shepherdesses that never existed but in the fancy of poets, while happy, glorious England affords, through a long course of centuries, examples of all that is lovely, good, and illustrious.

The terrific, which comes first in our order of division, is perhaps the highest species of subject in our art, requiring the greatest degree of talent to insure success in attempting it. It must be drawn from the mind, and in such instances, the manual skill of the artist, though indispensable, is a matter of inferior consideration. The daring hand that aims at these great objects often steps beyond the boundaries of human nature, and in its most successful achievement has but a hair's breadth escape of becoming ridiculous. An idea of danger, exhi-

bited or implied, is, I believe, invariably
necessary to the complete representation
of such subjects, and the action implying
or expressing the danger should always
be in suspense, or unaccomplished, that,
in the spectator's mind, anxiety and hope
may be united with terror. I know of no
instance more precisely illustrative of my
conception, than that of the two mothers
before the sagacious King of the Jews.
The imploring tenderness of the real
parent, added to the appearance of an
uplifted scimitar ready to fall on the destined child, makes the picture completely
an object of sublimity and terror, capable
of penetrating the deepest recesses of the
spectator's heart. But there are many
who, not content to work these magical
effects by the ample means which nature
never denies to those that seek them, try
to dash at once into sublimity, by intro-

ducing ghosts and goblins into their pictures. I confess I have insuperable objections to this sort of bombast in painting;
for a sprite or a goblin pourtrayed by those
even who have devoted their whole lives
to such representations, is nothing but a
human figure discoloured or distorted,
and on the unbiassed mind will produce
no sensation but that of disgust.

· Teniers, in some of his pictures of the
mock sublime, has given a most happy
illustration, in representing a sprite with
his nose protruded to such a length, that
it is converted into an oboe on which he
plays. If you attempt this ghostly kind
of ·sublime at all, I am persuaded you
should not wish to carry it farther than it
has been carried by a lady, distinguished
by her high rank, but still more distinguished by her exquisite taste and skill in

the practice of painting in water-colours.
You are, no doubt, acquainted with her
elegant designs to embellish an English
translation of the horrible German poem
of Leónora. But I cannot consistently
advise *you* to attempt any species of the
terrific in painting. To excel in it at
all, requires a great variety of knowledge,
the acquirement of which would be inconsistent with your other pursuits, as well as
with the delicacy of your feelings. You
must therefore leave to professors, who
cover canvas by the acre, the task of
calling up " spirits from the vasty deep,"
or of setting immeasurable ghosts *astride*
on the " blue summits of streamy Dun-
larvon." These remarks, however, though
intended to dissuade you from the attempt,
will, perhaps, also assist your judgments
in viewing the works of those who have
had the boldness to make it.

Our next subdivision is the grand; and here I may properly advise you to indulge your inclination, if it lead that way. In this all the parts should be broad and simple, both as to the whole, taken together, and as to the composition of each figure. The *number* of figures should, I think, in general, be few; though two very celebrated painters of the Italian school have fixed the least number at twelve, and the greatest at forty. It appears to me ridiculous to make limitations on this point, because, indisputably, many sublime effects have been produced in pictures, by the skilful exhibition of one or two figures only, and we have many instances in which the sublimity of a composition has suffered nothing by being extended to fifty or a hundred. But in treating subjects of the grand kind, in which the objects are unavoidably numerous, great art must be employed so to arrange them, and so to manage the direction of light, that those figures which, though necessary, are of lesser importance, may be melted into masses of shadow, or may contribute to extend and carry off the masses of light. I can conceive the grandest effect to be produced by wild scenery displayed round the dignified, yet solitary, figure of *him who cried aloud in the wilderness;* and I can suppose an effect equally grand, in a skilful representation of the same high character, surrounded by a *multitude,* to whom he delivers his sublime doctrine.

The leading events of our sacred history will afford you numerous subjects of this kind; and in advising you to attempt them, I conceive it no deviation at all from the advice I have before given you, to be guided by patriotism alone in the choice of your subjects: everything that is connected with the history of our faith, or that has contributed to its complete establishment, makes a part of our nearest and most important concerns. The simple, yet majestic, habiliments of the Jews are highly favourable to the breadth of drapery, so essential to grandeur, and the great decision of character observable in the elders and chiefs of that interesting nation, becomes a powerful instrument of narration in the details of a picture.

In compositions drawn from this source, we may justly be allowed to introduce supernatural beings; because they were oftentimes *permitted* to assume human forms, for the purpose of communicating with mortals, and should *then* be characterised and distinguished only by their superior grace, benignity, and sweetness. This appears to me not to admit of dispute, and I think the painter who should, in such case, adorn these disguised celestials with a pair of wings, would have no excuse to offer, but that his feeble pencil had no other means of pointing out that they were not meant for mere mortals. The angels who came to Lot, to warn him of the threatened visitation, were mistaken for beautiful young men, and the angel that attended Tobias in his journey, appeared only as a hired servant, till the time arrived when he was permitted to discover himself.

I cannot help wishing to impress on your minds the opinion I entertain of the extreme impropriety, the folly, of any other attempts to represent in painting the inhabitants of the world of spirits. We can express, by this art, nothing but

what has been received into our minds
through the medium of our sense of seeing, and those materials are, of course, all
of them, impressions of visible objects.
We may combine those impressions differently from what we found them : we
may set a man's trunk on a horse's
shoulders; we may give the head of a
bat to the body of a grasshopper and the
wings of a butterfly, in order to call it a
fairy ; we may paint the figure of a tall,
thin man, his outstretched arm pointing,
with crooked finger, and colour it blue
or green, to ". make a ghost of it:" but
such combinations and such attempts are
beneath the dignified simplicity of genuine
art, and should, I think, be looked on as
the feverish wanderings of a delirious
brain.

The subjects that you will find abundantly spread through the *sacred volume,* are such as may exhibit every possible modification of the *grand* in painting; but those to be found in the Gospels are the most exquisite, approaching some-times to the highest point of awful grandeur, or, at others, displaying a pa-thos and feeling that penetrate and melt the heart. Yet in this sublime work, there is *one* subject that no artist should *dare* profane by the touch of his *unhal-lowed pencil:* it is the *sad catastrophe* which finished the mortal career of the only perfect *character* that ever existed amongst us. The *grandeur,* the *majestic sublimity* of this heart-piercing event, are heightened in our minds by the indis-tinctness and gloom which our sorrow throws around it, and which are unavoid-ably dissipated when we see the blessed

confirmation of our hope depicted on a
few square feet of canvas, or paper.

There is only another remark that I
wish to make on subjects taken from
Scripture-history, and that is, to point
out to you the great error that painters,
in general, have fallen into, in surrounding the heads of their principal characters
with a halo, or glory, and sometimes of
making the figure of the infant Christ
splendid with inherent light. Had these
circumstances taken place in the reality,
the Jews, though born to unbelief, must
have been convinced by the unceasing
miracle; and, if it was not to be found in
the reality, I see no better reason for allowing it in painting than for giving
wings to disguised angels.

Prolix as these observations may appear
to you, as making but a part of my sub-

ject, you will, I fear, yet find them short and insufficient when you come to carry them into practice. I would, therefore, beg leave to direct you for further information on painting Scripture-history, to a very ingenious, learned, and entertaining French work, entitled * *Erreur des Peintres.*

Our national history, to which all must look with pride and pleasure, will furnish innumerable subjects of grandeur for your pencils. You may recal to your minds, for this purpose, the heroic Boadicea, nobly exciting her countrymen to resist and punish the oppressions of a tyrannic invader, and, at last, resolving rather to die gloriously than to live without honour

* I presented a copy of this work to the Library of Reference in the Royal Institution.

and freedom ; you may recollect, also, the undaunted and dignified courage of Caractacus, struggling for the liberty of his country, and even appearing the greatest in the midst of misfortunes ; you may take up the pencil to depict the unconquerable fortitude of Margaret, subduing, by the majesty of her deportment, the lawless freebooter of the forest ; or, you may pourtray the innocent, suffering Catherine, repelling, with firmness, the false charges of her interested accusers.

But you will think it time that I should proceed to the next division in our arrangement ; that is, the elegant. And here, I doubt not, you will feel yourselves peculiarly at home; since Britain exhibits, at this time, innumerable examples of every species of personal beauty, of every modification of grace. You will have

little more to do, even for your representations of the events of other times,
than to copy the dignified and lovely
figures that surround you ; and could our
ancestors, of any period, feel a consciousness of your efforts, they would not, I believe, find themselves losers by the performance.   Here, however, I must advise
you to be *active and vigilant*, in your endeavours to separate that which is fashion-
able from that which is really elegant
and graceful; and here, also, it may not
be improper to describe to you what I
understand by grace and by elegance.
Elegance, I take to signify that intricate
combination and contrast of lines in the
form of a figure which constitute an essential part of beauty : *grace*, I think,
must be understood to signify the same
kind of combination and contrast, not de-

16

pending on actual conformation, but arising out of the effects of motion. Thus a form, *not elegant in a quiescent state*, may become highly *graceful* in moving, by the influence of a superior intellect directing its motions; and thus, a figure may be *elegant* that is not graceful. Where these properties are united, they spread round the fortunate possessor a charm, a fascination, that nothing can resist.

In the inventions of fashion, which make beauty subservient to promote the manufacturing and commercial interests of the country, much is to be rejected, because founded in absolute deformity, both as to figure and dress. Therefore, in representing, by your pencils, the transactions and events of ages far back in our history, though you may properly repre-

Q

sent all the beauty, and elegance, and grace, of these polished times, you should, I think, be very cautious in introducing its fashions.

I need not remark to an audience so highly educated, that every period in our history is distinguished by a variation in its *modes and habits,* or in its *costume,* with those who prefer foreign words to sterling English. This, however, becomes a matter of serious study, to such of you as shall wish to paint correctly any one of the interesting events furnished by. our chronicles. Yet the sources from which you may derive this sort of knowledge are numerous, and easily accessible; and to those who have little leisure for minute research on such points, the very elaborate writings of Mr. Strutt will be powerful auxiliaries.

But, having gone thus far, I must, painful as the task may be, endeavour to warn
you against that affectation of *grace*, splendour, and variety, both as to forms and
colours, which pervades the works of some
of the few who have, at this time, any
claims to merit for painting figures in
water-colours. It was justly remarked,
some years ago, by Sir Joshua Reynolds,
that, *in his time*, the practice of contrasting the forms and limbs of figures was
carried to such an excess, that he almost
judged it necessary to lay the rule on the
other side. Were he *now* to come amongst
us, enlightened as he was by science and
taste, and to witness the contortions, dis-
tortions, and even dislocations, that are·
admitted, under the idea of giving grace,
he would be astonished and confounded.
Grace is ever simple, wholly incompatible

with over-strained action; and colour, in the hands of a skilful and scientific practitioner, aims not to dazzle, but to gratify, the sight, by delicate contrasts, and imperceptible gradations.

There are some respects, I must acquaint you, in which compositions of the *elegant kind* are attended with more difficulty than either the terrific or the grand; it is when considered as matters of narration. As they are not susceptible of violent emotions, or of rapid and boisterous action, they require to be marked by a more accurate delineation of countenance, by a more judicious and attentive selection in the accompaniments. The *terrific* demands the association of huge mountains, foaming torrents, or impending dangers; the *grand* calls for the accompanying aid of wild forests, massy rocks, and stupenduous architecture ; the *elegant* requires to be placed in cultivated landscapes, embellished apartments, or splendid palaces. There should, besides this, be some appropriate circumstance of person or thing, to point out the event you meant to exhibit, as distinct from any other for which it might else be mistaken.

We come now to the *rural*, as the last division in our arrangement, and, though it may perhaps be truly said that subjects of this kind do *not* excite any of the stronger passions, it must be admitted that they are more favourable than all the rest to picturesque representation. The natural gracefulness of deportment which we see in some of the rustics of this kingdom, particularly those of Westmoreland and Cumberland, the combinations that arise out of

their employments and pastimes, the forms
of their implements, and the neatness of
the style of their attire, all unite with our
invariable attachment to rural life, to
render such subjects a source of the most
lively and unceasing interest. The short,
yet elegantly pathetic, poem of Gray, written in a *country* church-yard, has many
beautiful pictures of this kind, though
perhaps none more strikingly beautiful
than that of the children, who

> —— " run to lisp their sire's return,
> Or climb his knee, the envied kiss to share."

The Shepherd's Week of Gay, and
the incomparable works of Thomson,
will also add greatly to your stock of materials ; and you have one great advantage
in subjects of this kind, that the originals
are either constantly at hand, or to be
easily procured.

My duty here compels me to point out
to you a disease which has attacked this
branch of art so powerful as almost to have
undermined the judgments of some of our
best performers, and will have no remedy,
that I know of, but in your determination
to discountenance it; I mean the constant
desire of making what are called *pretty
faces.* It is not that I would offer an objection to any one introducing the highest
degree of possible beauty into his pictures,
for to look on even the semblance of human beauty is one of the greatest enjoy-
ments of our life. The female rustics in
our farms and villages are oftentimes
lovely to a high degree, and in such compositions as properly admit them, I would
have that loveliness copied to the utmost
stretch of the art; but my objection is to
setting bad imitations of Greek and Ro-

man faces on the shoulders of English peasants, to seeing the same set of features constantly forced on our sight in every character, and called *pretty*, because the eyes are large, the cheeks *red*, and the mouth tucked up into an unmeaning simper.

Taking it, now, for granted that you have agreed to separate in your minds and in your practice the light and shadow from the colouring of your pictures and drawings, and to suppose, during the first part of your process, all the objects you mean to imitate as wholly divested of colour, your first * operation will be, to shadow the parts that are turned from the light, or from which the light is in-

* This process, it is trusted, will be fully explained by the plates which accompany this Lecture.

tercepted; your second proceeding will be, to express the different degrees of light on the surfaces that are in light; and your third will be, to express in the shadows of the first class those darker shadows which are occasioned by reflected light. Your performance is thus ready for colouring; and I beg leave to repeat that we are now referring to complexion only, or, in the technical language of painters, to the colouring of the *carnations*. Your first attention, then, must be directed to express the blue or grey tints, which you will do with a mixture of the finest carmine, and genuine Antwerp blue: many artists employ for this purpose a composition of ultramarine and vermillion, which is highly objectionable, as I shall shew you at a fit opportunity. These greys must be distinguished into local and accidental, observing that the former will be almost of a pure blue. The local greys are those made by the thinness of the skin shewing the larger veins through it ; for any dark colour, even red, when seen through a light-coloured semi-transparent medium, assumes an appearance of grey or blue ; and this effect is beautifully celebrated by Mr. Hayley, when he speaks of those dazzling complexions, in which

> —— " the blue meand'ring vein
> Sheds a soft lustre thro' the lucid snow."

In every face you will find the local grey invariably between the eyes and the nose, and in the passage from the outer extremity of the eye-brow across the temple to the hair : in very young persons the former is the most obvious ; in elderly persons, the latter becomes most perceptible, encreasing greatly with extreme age. The accidental greys are those which are to be found in all complexions at the edges of the shadows, and which have been supposed, by most painters, to be grey only. by contrast, as occupying a medium place between the vivid colour of the lights, and the grosser colour of the shadows. But this I believe to be a mistake. The appearance of grey is actual, and arises from part of the shaded side of the solid flesh shewing through the enlightened part of the skin. The breadth of this grey will therefore be in proportion to the thickness of the skin, and to the position of the spectator with regard to the direction of light. It cannot appear at all unless more be seen of the light than of the shaded side of the object. If the shadow of the flesh and of the skin

coincide to the eye, then the edge of the
shadow exhibits no alteration but the mere
diminution of its force; but if more be
seen of the shaded than of the enlightened side of the object, *then* the edge of
the shadow will be of a brighter hue than
its general tint; because part of the enlightened surface of the flesh will shew
through the shadow of the skin.

To express truly these accidental greys,
you will take the colours already prescribed, and pass the mixture along the
edges of your first shadow, softening it
off both ways, so as to become an intermediate gradation between that and the
second, observing always that it be kept
lighter than the general tone of the first
shadows. Your next step will then be to
give the reds or reddish tints to your subject, which you will do invariably with

Chinese vermillion and carmine. Having thus far prepared the ground-work of your figure, you will take a mixture of carmine or of Venetian red and gamboge, of each according to the complexion of man, or woman, you have to represent, and cover the whole of the shadows, colours and all, except the balls of the eyes and the shining lights on the forehead and nose, which, on a very fine skin, will be perfectly white by the quantity of light they reflect.   When this shall have been accomplished, you will add the tints of the reflex lights and colours, as described in my last Lecture, and make such further variations in the local colour as your subject, when duly examined, will suggest; which will in general be a partial augmentation of the reds, and a repetition occasionally of the general colour, though

somewhat yellower, to serve as an intermediate between the general colour and
the reds. This brings your work to a
conclusion under the idea of a tinted
drawing, as I have already defined it; and
a few experiments will convince you that
this mode of proceeding affords the most
ample means of imitating nature truly
and expeditiously; that it is capable of
great delicacy, and that it is also capable
of great clearness, force, and brilliancy.
If you wish to make pictures of your performances, you will then carry them
through this process of colouring after
the first and second shadows, and then
add the local colour to the proper proportion of Indian-ink for finishing the shadows, adding carmine and Venetian-red
to the last touches in those shadows of
the third class, where the light, passing

through a thin part of the flesh, takes and imparts the colour of the medium. But this last circumstance should be considered and treated with great caution; for it has been the inducement to innumerable errors amongst painters, particularly those of the present times. The eye-lids, the thin parts of the nose, the mouth, and even the fingers, when opposed to a very strong light, will, from this cause, exhibit a great degree of redness in their respective shadows: but it never can follow from these circumstances that we should plaister them with pure vermillion, or that we should carry this flaming military colour into the cavities of the ears, to the shadow under the throat, and indeed to the last touches in every part of the undraped human figure. I entreat you to weigh this in your minds,

to look around you on the various pictures each day will presént to your observation, and, when you shall have discovered any of these daring violations of
truth, to set them down in your memories
as quicksands you ought to shun.

The process I have now had the honour of describing to you, is founded in
a close observation of Nature; and I trust,
if you give it due consideration, you will
be convinced that it is calculated to lead,
by the most simple means, to the happiest
and most successful results. I will therefore venture to hope that, as your subjects
are chosen, your materials pointed out,
and the process of using them circum-
stantially described, some of you at least
will put them soon in a state of active
operation.

To those who wish for a process for

15

copying old pictures with certainty, I have recommended the use of water-colours. The practitioner will prepare his copy as already described, to the end of the second shadow and local colours, being more or less deep in the tones, according to the original. He will then wash the whole over with Venetian-red and gamboge, to the colour of the highest light of his model ; reinforce the local colours, where they appear too weak, and then finish the whole with a mixture of such browns, or brown and blue, as appears to have been employed in the shadows of the original picture. When finished, the copy should be four or five times covered with isinglass, dissolved in spirit of wine *, and the

* As this is difficult to prepare, I have given the receipt to Hastings, in the Haymarket, and to Barker, in Oxford-street, who have it ready for sale.

R

result may be illusive: I once saw one of
the first judges in England deceived for
half an hour by a copy of this kind,
though he had the original in his other
hand at the same time.

But after leading you through this view
of the modes into which you may divide
your subjects of figures, and the manner of
colouring their complexions, I must call
your attention to another branch of the
study, which is of the highest importance ;
it is *expression*, not merely of countenance,
though certainly the most considerable,
but also of gesture and deportment, as
indicating the affections and movements
of the human mind. This is important
to make painting intellectual ; and yet we
have authority to believe, that the antient
Greek painters practised their art very
long, and even with applause, before any
attempt was made by them to give the

least appearance of expression to the countenances of their figures. It would require the whole of a long lecture to discuss this part of my subject with that discriminating attention to which it is justly entitled; but that not being permitted me, I will endeavour to give you some leading principles to assist your pursuit. It cannot, I trust, be thought too much to require from those who wish to excel in this most interesting department of the painter's art, that they should devote a short time to acquire some knowledge of the construction of the human head, and of the forms of the muscles in the human face, by which the features are moved in different directions. This knowledge being obtained and digested, daily observations on nature, and on the works of art, which are so numerous in

every part of this country, will lead you
to remark what muscles are employed,
and in what degree to express such or
such different emotions of the mind; and
every remark so made will become a rule
of future practice. But great care must be
taken to distinguish between a sudden
emotion and the expression of the same
feeling when continued and fixed. The
sudden joy that irradiates a countenance,
and gives the most pleasing activity to
every feature, presents, if long continued,
no indications but of a settled cheerfulness : the burst of sudden grief, the pangs
of sudden despair, contract and depress
the features to all the evidences of mental
agony ; but the same cause continuing for
a length of time, the whole face relaxes
into gloomy languor and pallid stillness.
You have, however, much more to con-

sider than all this; for, in a skilfully-exe-
cuted picture, every limb, every joint of
a figure should speak the same language
as the features. If the emotions expressed be tumultuous and violent, the
action of the person will be rapid and extended, and the objects which excited
them, or those to which they tend, should,
if possible, be introduced, except in the
case of *insanity*, where the cause being
remote, and the tendency variable and
uncertain, neither can properly be admitted.

But to the *dilettante* artist, I would in
general recommend the choice of such
subjects as depend for their interest on
the representation of the softer workings
of the heart and mind, as love, tenderness,
and entreaty. In delicate love, the countenance is serene but glowing, the eyes

quite open to gaze on the object, and the attitude or motion graceful and gentle. In the expression of tenderness, the gaze is less ardent, and somewhat mixed with solicitude, the attitude bending towards its object, or leaning over it.　In entreating and beseeching, the eye is fully open, the brow a little contracted to shew anxiety; the mouth apparently speaking, the figure turned towards the person addressed, and the object in request should if possible be exhibited.

These few rules, and their modifications, will serve to remove your difficulty in very many cases; but when you shall require to enter further into the subject, I would advise you to consult the very able Treatise by Gerarde Lairesse, which I have mentioned in a former Lecture; and, also, a very ingenious work, published by Mr. Bell, on the Anatomy of Expression in Painting.

The next time I shall be permitted to address you, it will be for the purpose of applying the process described in my last Lecture, to the practice of drawing and painting landscape. I shall then have a new opportunity of pointing out advantages which painting in water-colours possesses over every process as yet known.

LECTURE V.

In my discourse of to-day I shall have the honour to direct your attention to the consideration of landscape-painting.

This branch of the art, so delightful to those who practice it, may be divided into the grand, the elegant, and the rural. The terrific, which we had occasion to consider not many days ago, is not within the scope of mere landscape-painting: it necessarily requires the introduction of figures to describe the impression of impending danger, so indispensable in this

class of subjects. From this view only,
were there no other grounds for such an
opinion, it will be evident, that compositions of figures are one degree, at least,
higher in point of dignity than the finest
landscapes. The *grand* in landscape requires that the forms should be large and
massy, and the situation should, if possible,
be so chosen as to exclude the access of a
general or diffusive light. To obtain this
effect, the morning or evening light should
generally be selected, when even diminu-
tive objects afford broad and ample shadows, and when the quantity of vapour,
either rising or descending, by concealing
or softening the minutiæ of the scene,
contributes much to the idea of vastness.
But the sources from which you will draw
the most powerful aids in subjects of this
kind, are those splendid or awful effects of

atmosphere which are transient, nay, often momentary; yet which can, notwithstanding, fill the most capacious mind with sensations of majesty and sublimity. To illustrate this part of my subject more fully, I would beg leave to refer you to the unrivalled compositions of our inimitable Wilson: his Solitude, his Niobe, his Ceyx and Alcione, his Meleagar, all well known, at least by the engravings after them, afford perfect models for the various modes of grandeur in landscape. From these you will infer, that a principal source of grandeur, in your subjects of this class, is the introduction of such circumstances as imply rapid and violent motion, or the probable occurrence of danger. The convulsions of an earthquake, that cleaves huge mountains to their centre; the howling wind, that bends or tears up every herb

and tree in its progress; the dashing tor-
rent, that falls, foaming, from rock to rock
down the mountain's side, are objects from
which your landscapes will derive some of
their most powerful effects.

The elegant in landscape includes, I
conceive, all those scenes in which art has
been successfully employed, or in which
the happy combinations of smiling nature
seem to have left nothing for taste to
desire. Such subjects naturally look to
architecture as the appropriate source of
ornament for them. The noble mansion,
that becomes the dwelling of merited
opulence, or of hereditary honour; the
fragrant garden, or shrubbery, where expence and taste have united to exhibit in
one view, round the supposed temple of
some sylvan deity, the beauties of many
climates; the ivy-covered walls and

mouldering columns that once enclosed monastic societies ; are all fit subjects for the embellishment of elegant landscape.

The sky, in general, with subjects of elegant landscape, should be open and tranquil, and, though the golden rays of the departing sun may sometimes be allowed to gleam through the fretted windows, or along the deserted ailes of an ecclesiastic ruin; yet the retirements of greatness and wealth should, I think, always be shown in that splendour of full meridian light which vivifies all nature, and seems emblematic of the prosperity on which it shines.

Rural landscape is more ample in its range; and is, perhaps, most of all the three kinds suited for the dilettante artist: its subjects may be extensive or limited, either embracing the whole valley, with the various occupations and pursuits of husbandmen, swains, and village-maids, or detailing, with light but faithful hand, the broken style, the mud-built cottage, or the slender plank that forms a bridge over the willow-covered stream. In rural scenes, however, of this latter kind, composed of few objects, and those near at hand, it must not be forgotten, that more than half the beauty, and nearly the whole interest, arises from that truth of imitation which it has lately been very much the custom to decry, as beneath the dignity of a great artist. Each tree, each little flower, demands its appropriate touch of the pencil; the fibrous roots, hanging over the edge of a mouldering bank, the fractures in a piece of shattered railing, the weather-beaten thatch, and even the bits of moss that enliven it, the crumbling plaster that shows the rude stone of a cottage, all become sources of picturesque effect in the hands of a performer who has accustomed himself to render things in painting as they really appear, not as he thinks they ought to be. Many of the pictures of Ruysdale, some of those of Decker, as well as a few of the pictures of Hobbema, afford delightful specimens of such subjects as I would arrange in the most pleasing class of rural landscape. I am anxious to recommend, in the strongest manner, this style of rural landscape to your particular study; because we have, every where around us, the most ample materials for such combinations. . The trees in our valleys are highly luxuriant, and the continual changes of atmosphere they experience, give them a variety of form and character, truly picturesque, and

never to be found, except in an insular
situation; but, in addition to this, there is
no country existing that exhibits a greater
variety in the mode of constructing its
rural dwellings than Britain. In the
south, and in the midland counties, where
stone is not so easily procured, the habit-
ation of the peasant is formed of mud and
timber; in both nearly on the same principle; while, in the south, the mildness of
the climate covers every little hut with a
profusion of blooming and fragrant flowers.
In the neighbourhood of the metropolis,
even where the traces of art are observable in the precision of almost every build-
ing, there are many little circumstances of
decoration which make the lesser dwellings highly favourable to the representation of the pencil. In some of the counties of the north, where unceasing labour

is required to counteract the unkindness
of a climate that produces corn sparingly,
but stone in abundance, the cottages are
generally formed of irregular stones, piled
on each other; frequently without any
kind of cement; but their inartificial construction, the various kinds of shelter they
oppose to the storms that often deluge
them, and their wisely chosen scite on the
verdant bank of some silvery stream, render them, most truly, picturesque and
interesting objects.

This, too, is the style of landscape, that
connects itself, more than any other, with
the drawing and painting of figures, the
style wherein each may bear such a proportion in the picture, as to be necessary
to the effect and understanding of the
other.   The figures, however, that are introduced, should be the genuine tenants

of the scene, in form, in feature, and in habiliments, characterizing the district, and even the particular county.

Having thus classed the subjects for your study and practice in landscape, I would proceed to remark on the materials, which contribute to its combinations and effects. The most extensive of these, and the most difficult to understand, or to represent truly, is air.

The atmosphere which we breathe, and which is interposed between our sight and every object, is transparent, in a greater or less degree, according to the quantity of vapour with which it is loaded, or the position in which we stand with regard to the light. We find that glass, and even chrystal or diamonds, may be so doubled and redoubled, as not to allow the possibility of distinguishing objects through the

s

medium; because the particles that compose them, though pervious to light in a very great degree, are also susceptible of a certain portion of shadow. It is even so with the atmosphere, the thinnest and most transparent of all media. That it is capable of obstructing the passage of light, we see evidently in the circumstance, that when the air is highly illuminated by the sun, and we stand with our backs to the light, distant objects of any kind are scarcely discernible, because we see the enlightened sides of the particles that compose the medium. To illustrate this, if you will look, from the street, in a sunny day at any house on which the light strongly falls, you will find that you can see no object that may be in the rooms through the windows, unless it be placed near the glass, which is not the case with the same

windows on a cloudy day. If, then, the
particles of air can obstruct and reflect
light, they must also be liable to have
their shadows : taking, therefore, the particles of lights and shadows, or of black and
white, the colour of atmosphere will be
grey, varying a little as the one or the
other principle predominates. Now, this
being admitted, I have further to remark,
that, as this medium, through which we
see every thing, has thus in itself an appearance of colour, its effect in landscape
is to make lighter every thing that is darker than its colour, and to darken every
thing that is lighter ; till, each approaching
the other, the objects become so many
flat skreens, and at last, from a continuance
of the same cause, totally disappear. This
is a point so exceeding clear in itself, and
so easily demonstrated by the most simple

experiments, that I could almost suppose
it had never been doubted ; yet, one of
the most, esteemed landscape painters this
'country has produced *, laid it down as a
principle, and constantly practised upon
it, that the interposition of the air makes
all objects lighter, and that therefore the
lightest part of the sky in a picture must
be lighter than any object in the landscape.
His mode of producing his pictures,
founded in this idea, was to paint the
sky first, and then, with broad flat
tints of grey, to lay in the different masses
of distances, making each darker as approaching nearer to the foreground.   On
the respective flat skreens, he then expressed as much of the detail of parts as it
was his custom to allow, always keeping,

* This Artist is not now living.

in the light objects, the same relative proportion of tone established by the first
broad masses. This would be true, if all
the objects, in all the distances, were actually in shadow, because they are then
darker than the colour of the atmosphere,
and must consequently be made successively lighter by its interference; but
the artist, who evidently mistook a partial
operation for a general principle, constantly made all his objects throw their
respective shadows as if in the strongest
sun-shine. To satisfy your minds that I
am not misleading you, I beg the favour
of you, in the first opportunity of a bright
day, to take a piece of paper or any white
object, and, standing full in the light,
bring the paper in apparent contact with
the whitest cloud you can find in the sky.
You will perceive, in a moment, that the

paper is many distinct degrees whiter
than the cloud. This, therefore, will, I
hope, be sufficient on this point, which I
should have but slightly mentioned, were
it not that the doctrine I have just dis-
proved has many powerful followers, both
in theory and in practice.

I have shown you that the colour of
atmosphere is grey, and the cause of it.
I have now to remind you, that the vast
empyrean of the sky, which we consider
as blue, is so only by contrast with the
vivid and powerful tones and colours,
that cover the whole face of nature in a
brilliant day; it is simply an effect of
white over black, producing a grey; or
of the darkness of infinite space, seen
through the enlightened medium of the
air that surrounds us. This is not difficult to prove. M. de Saussure informs
us, and the same testimony is given by

Bourrit and others, that on the summits
of the highest Alps, where the air is so
thin as to be scarcely respirable, the sky,
over-head, appears nearly black; the experience of every night convinces us that
the sky is not then blue, and that it is
more and more black as there is less
light on the globe to give it an apparent
colour by comparison. But, to give you a
more convincing proof, I beg you to take
any kind of tube, of which the inside is painted black, and apply it to the
clearest part of the sky, in the clearest
summer's day. You will then perceive
that, by shutting out from your sight
every other object that could be the
means of contrast, that which you thought
blue has ceased to appear so, and seems
nothing but a mixture of white and black.
This examination, while it furnishes us a

s 4

most important fact for consideration,
convinces us of the littleness, the insuffi-
ciency of art, when compared to the great
operations of nature. I have stated to
you before, the great deficiency of painting, with regard to its powers, both of
light and of dark: I have now to remind
you of its wonderful incompetency in
splendour of colours, when compared with
the appearances of nature. It must be
evident to you, from the remarks I have
already made, that the powerful tones
and vivid colours, displayed in natural
landscape, make, by comparison, the black
and white of the atmosphere, and the sky
appear decidedly blue. The ingenuous
Count Rumford has proved also, the possibility of accomplishing the same by
artificial contrasts with colours ; but, to
do this, he found it necessary to employ

the utmost extent of a painter's means, which would be totally incompatible with the beautiful gradations that appear in nature. Thus, circumscribed as to our means of operation, in endeavouring to follow the mode by which the effects we wish to imitate are produced, the only consideration that remains for us, is how best to supply the deficiency.

It has ever been an object of solicitude with me, to establish, for the advancing practitioner, some mode of proceeding so nearly approaching to the philosophical effect, (the rational proceeding of nature, in producing her appearances,) that a certain degree of truth of representation should be more than probable, and that any serious deviation should be almost impossible. These important advantages, I have long been convinced, are to be found

only in the highest degree of tinted drawing. We will therefore proceed to consider that method, as applied to subjects
of landscape, which I had the honour of
explaining to you in my third Lecture, as
applied to figures. It has been shown
that positive shadow is black, that lesser
degrees of shadow are modifications of
black, and that the local colour of an object, in its shadowed surfaces, differs so
much from the colour of its enlightened
surfaces, as is equal to the degree of local
colour, added to the proportion of black
which constitutes the shadow. This is
true to the greatest nicety, as applied to
objects near the spectator, as subjects of
figures are generally supposed to be;
but, in subjects of landscape, where the
objects are successively removed to greater
and greater distances from the eye, the
interposition of atmosphere between the

spectator and the objects viewed, begins
by diminishing the appearance of local
colour in the shadows, compared with the
appearance of the lights, till at last the
colour of the objects appears in the enlightened parts only; which also degrade,
by the same cause still operating, till the
most remote distance becomes a mass of
neutral colour, somewhat darker than the
atmosphere near it. It might be presumed, therefore, from these deductions,
that covering the near objects with their
local colour, added to the colours occasioned by reflected light, and regularly
diminishing the force of the local colour
as the objects are meant to recede, would
give the truth of natural appearances;
because shadow is grey, or a modification
of black and white, and atmosphere acts
on the same principle. But it has been
shown, that the splendour of colours in

nature converts, by comparison, this grey into positive blue or very nearly so, and we have no such power of contrast in painting. We are, therefore, reduced to the necessity of employing blue to represent what in nature is only a mixture of black and white, and, from these facts, taken together, results what I now propose to you.

Having obtained the real, and nothing more than the real, light and shadow of your landscape with Indian ink, you will then begin to colour from the sky, the shaded parts of the clouds being presumed to have been inserted with the material used for the other shadows. The clear empyrean of the sky will be given with indigo, or with Prussian blue, or with Prussian blue over indigo, according to the state of atmosphere meant to be represented. This same blue must be afterwards distributed over the whole of the extreme distance, and continued on the shadows of the other distances, diluting the tone as the objects may be supposed nearer to the eye, till it disappear at that part near the foreground, where atmosphere must be considered as not having a visible effect. After this preparation, if the local colours and reflected lights be given on the principle I have already described, the result will be, with a judicious practitioner, a true resemblance to the nature he means to represent, and, in the hands of one almost a novice, the production will at least be tolerable. This must be understood, as I have stated it, as applying it to tinted drawing, which I am persuaded should be the first mode of study for any one who wishes afterwards to paint his

subjects, in whatever manner or process.
If you wish to make *pictures* in water-
colours of your landscapes, then the mode
of proceeding is a little different, though
resting on the same philosophical reasoning. You will, after a correct outline,
begin with the blue of the sky; you will
mix Indian ink with the blue for the
shadows of the clouds, and, in advancing
to the foreground, you will add to a portion of the local colour so much Indian
ink as would constitute the tone of the
shadow of each object, had it been white.
The local colour should then be generally
distributed upon the objects, with the re-
serve, as to distance, which I have just
mentioned, and afterwards those colours
which appear by reflection in the landscape, and by refraction in the sky. Advanced to this state, your picture is ready

14

for finishing from the distance to the foreground, which commences by retouching
the shadows of the remote objects with
the blue of the sky, and, nearer, mixing
the Indian ink with each local colour for
finishing the shadowed objects or surfaces
till the whole be completed. I would
wish, most earnestly, to recommend to
your notice and adoption, this truly
rational mode of proceeding, in opposition
to that which is much practised at present, of taking up colours at once, and
arranging them, by no other guide than
the visual susceptibility of the teacher or
the pupil.

But if, by preference, you paint your
landscapes in oil-colours, a different mode
of proceeding must be resorted to, less
simple and less demonstrative, as to the
truth of its effects, but indispensable to

the kind of material. You will draw out
your subject correctly on the pannel
or canvass, not with chalk, but with a
black-lead pencil, inserting in your outline the figures, and other moveable objects, by which you mean to embellish
the scene; and, in painting the different
parts subsequently, you will recollect to
paint round these objects, so that when
it comes to their turn to be expressed,
they may be executed on the canvass, and
not on the colours of such parts as make
their back ground. The reason of this I
have stated before, though not as applying
precisely to this case. When, in oil painting, a light colour is put over a dark one,
the inevitable consequence is, that, in
time, the dark colour will become evident
through the other, and the light object
will seem to sink into the ground. The

circumstance is perfectly well known; and we see instances of its unfortunate effects in the landscapes of some of the greatest masters, who have chosen to finish their scenery first, and then introduce the figures. You will begin with the sky, and next take the distance, both of which should, if possible, be finished at one sitting. These should be painted very thin in most parts, and no substance of colour allowed any where but in the highest lights. I have advised you before to paint your oil-pictures invariably on a white-ground; but, in this department, it is even of more importance to do so than in any other. For the certain change of colour, resulting from the nature of oil, will soon lower the tone of the light parts, and, if the canvass be of a dark colour, that colour will shew more and more

T

through by time, greatly increasing the degradation, and totally destroying the clearness so necessary to the appearance of air. There is no way, as yet discovered, of counteracting this unfortunate tendency of oils, but by painting the light parts of such pictures very thinly on a white sur-face. The middle and foregrounds of your subjects will be taken next after the distance, dividing them generally into the masses of light and dark, and leaving the extremes of each principle to be inserted in the finishing. You will mix, in the shadowed parts of the middle distance, always a certain portion of the grey, by which you have represented the effect of atmosphere in the sky and in the most remote parts ; and paint the foreground and near objects, excepting in the highest lights, as much as possible with thin and transparent colours. This advice applies particularly to the painting of the trees, and, above all, to such parts of them as come against a light part of the sky, or as shew the effect of light, passing through the foliage. The pictures of Claude Lorraine are painted with very thin colour in every part, except the prominent parts of the foregrounds; the best pictures of Ruysdale are painted with transparent colours, excepting the shining lights; the pictures of our own incomparable Gainsborough are executed nearly in the same manner; as are also the finest works of Wilson; and the tasteful landscapes of Mr. Abbott, of Exeter, which are almost equal to any others, owe a great part of their beauty to a similar treatment. Attempts have lately been made by an oil-painter of high celebrity, to paint land-

scape scenery in two colours, representing
the light and shadow, and then glazing
the objects over with their local tints; but
owing to the causes which I described to
you in a former Lecture, when discussing
the same practice as applied to painting
figures, such attempts have not succeeded.
Allow me to suggest to such of you as
wish to paint landscape in oils, a mode of
proceeding which will be attended with
great success: it has been tried, as yet, I
believe, but by one artist. Having drawn
your subject correctly on a white paper,
properly stretched, you will execute the
sky and distance in transparent water-colours, finishing, as highly as possible, and
then varnish the whole with isinglass varnish. Upon this you will paint the
middle parts and the foregrounds with
oil colours, only observing to paint the

extreme lights, in such parts, of a very
high tone, perhaps a little above the truth,
as compared to the sky and distance, because the oil-colours will become darker,
while those parts of the picture which have
been executed in water, will remain the
same. In this practice you will unite the
acknowledged advantages of both kinds
of painting, and I am persuaded, your
satisfaction, on the result, will more than
recompense the labour.

There is a general defect in the practice
of engraving trees, which defect is also to
be found in the trees of such of our landscape painters as pride themselves on
what is called *pencilling* — it is in representing all the leaves of their trees as if
they were seen with the flat surface constantly presented to the eye ; though it is
evident, without much consideration, that

the leaves of a tree, unless when strongly
blown by the wind, must be seen in an
infinite variety of directions, and consequently appear of as many different
shapes.

The first material of landscape to which
I would direct your attention, is the various kinds of vegetation which serve to
clothe the surface of the earth, without
concealing its form. All this I would
wish to class under the term herbage.
The proper treatment of herbage in drawings and paintings of landscape, is by no
means unimportant, though frequently
little attended to; much of the truth of
representation depends upon it. In the
most distant parts, a faint and even tint
will generally be sufficient: as we approach
nearer, stronger tints, with the proper
variations of colour, will be required; but

14

as we advance to the foreground, something more must be done: Roughness
then begins to appear, and must be expressed, or truth will vanish, and the part,
on which the roughness ought to be visible, will, for the want of it, seem out of
its place. Still nearer, the indications
must be larger, and must take more decided forms, gradually changing, as they
approach, into touches of determined and
varied directions ; nearer still, indications
of form will appear, and, on the foreground itself, the grass must be represented by long, slender touches, so placed as
to express the manner of its growth, and
plants, and weeds of a larger description,
must be drawn, shaded, and coloured with
accuracy. I am aware that many persons
may start at the idea of a process, apparently so tedious, for those parts of a pic-

ture which they have been used to think
trivial, but it'will be found, in practice,
much less so than would be supposed.
The truth of the effect will, in its progressive appearance, be amusing to the performer, and the success of the execution,
particularly in detailing the foreground,
will, when duly considered, afford as much
delight, as the same success in those parts
which are usually deemed of more importance. You have, no doubt, frequently
seen and observed careless pictures of
lawns and fields, in which the grazing
cattle, exhibit their feet entirely, even to
the lowest edge of their hoof, because, if
the painter were to represent, in those
parts, the herbage that necessarily should
cover them, he would find himself inevitably compelled to bestow, on every other
part of his grounds, the indispensable at-

tention which I have now recommended
to you. To execute, with truth, a perfectly flat country, receding from the eye,
has been considered as a very difficult attainment in landscape-painting, and has,
when attained, been universally admired.
A regular diminution of the smaller details that cover the surface of the country,
both in their size and in their distinctness, will not fail to accomplish this; as
we may observe in some of the first pictures of Claude Lorraine, whom no artist
ever surpassed in his masterly expression
of such details. A similar attention to
this part of pencilling, with a more rapid
diminution of the parts as they recede
from the eye, will express with equal certainty, what cannot be expressed by any
other means, the effect of a view looking
down a steep hill, which has hitherto been
considered as almost impossible.

Trees are the material of landscape which
follow next in importance, and would merit
a long and close attention; but as the time
is limited during which I may be permitted to detain you, I shall confine myself
to remark on the distinguishing character
of those trees which are most frequently
to be met with in this country; and shall
endeavour to point out in what manner
they may be most advantageously introduced and employed in landscape.* Extensive woods, it is evident, can be introduced in the extreme distance only; the
tops of the trees appearing rounded, and
receding in perspective into the distance,
and subject to the same rules which I have

* My observations on this part of the subject have
been fully corroborated by the written communications
of a noble Earl, who is one of the best foresters in
Britain.

laid down for the herbage. Wherever
considerable masses of light and shadow
are required, young trees, if all, or mostly
of the same sort, and nearly of the same
age, must be rejected, as they are generally
straggling, and thinly clad with foliage:
in such cases, also, speaking generally,
the larch, the spruce, fir, and the silver
fir, must be refused. Trees, when approaching their full height, throw out shorter
annual shoots, and, becoming what is called
clump-headed, take a decided character
much more favourable to the pencil. That
each species of tree has a peculiar character in itself, cannot be doubted: this
character, whatever it be, pervades the
whole of it, trunk, ramification, bark, and
foliage. A proper attention to these circumstances will give to your compositions
an appearance, not only of truth, but of

variety, which is not to be attained by
other means. The knowledge, therefore,
of character in trees is indispensable, and
nothing will conduce so much to the
attainment of it, as beginning to copy
them from nature, during the season
when they are divested of leaves. The
trunk and ramification are then distinctly seen, and the species of sweep,
curve, or twist, which the branches take
in diverging from the trunk; and of the
smaller sprays in diverging from the
branches, (for it will be found the same
throughout,) may be accurately delineated
and got by heart. That particular touch,
which characterizes the foliage and the
bark of each tree, must be attended to,
as also the sort of shapes into which foliage, when luxuriant, naturally forms itself:
it will appear in different trees, either in

bunches hanging down, or like shelves
overhanging each other, or in tufts pointing
upwards, or in broad and swelling masses,
faintly sub-divided into smaller. There
is, perhaps, no better way of studying the
touch, proper for expressing different kinds
of foliage, than observing, in a clear summer's day, when the sun is high, the shadows thrown by the thin branches on any
smooth ground near them ; this will give
you on a large scale what you have only
to copy in a small. The alterations which
take place in trees, in consequence of their
age, must not be overlooked. In all, I
believe, the bark, in almost all the ramification, and in some few the appearance
of the foliage undergoes a change. The
progressive changes of the bark are observable at once, in the various parts of
the same tree : and the transition from one

to the other, is worthy of notice. Besides
these changes, trees are subject to many
others from accidents, and from circumstances of former or present situation.
Trees planted very close, and left so for
a considerable time, have few or no side-
branches, and some sorts have, and others
have not, the property of putting out side-
branches, when relieved from their con-
finement by the axe or by the tempest,
and are then more fit objects for the tim-
ber-merchant than the painter. Lopping
and pollarding, also produce wonderful
changes on the aspect of trees, sometimes
rendering them highly picturesque, and
sometimes disgusting; but always dispro-
portioned from their natural character.

The first of our indigenous trees for
picturesque effect, is indisputably the oak,
and that in every stage of its growth.

The bark, when young, is of a clear and
glossy colour, interspersed with rough
touches, the remains of decayed twigs ;
its growth is upright and spreading.
When full grown, its trunk is strong and
massy, its bark rough and furrowed, its
limbs large and angular, and branching
off from the stem in such a manner, that
it is difficult to ascertain where the stem
ends, and where the branches begin. The
general direction of its lower limbs is
horizontal; of those nearer to the top
more upwards; but owing to its angular
growth, which is visible even in the smallest sprays, hardly over perpendicular. Its
foliage is of a deep and strong, yet cheerful, green, when luxuriant, producing the
noblest masses ; and when thinly spread,
owing to its tufted manner of growth, and
its deep indented edges, it never appears

meagre. In spring, its young leaves are of
a yellowish olive tint ; its autumnal colour,
which comes on later than that of almost
any other tree, is a strong, yet lively reddish brown; for a short time after mid-
summer, its aspect is enlivened by a
second growth, of a paler green on the
deep tint of its first foliage : a peculiarity
also observable in the elm.   No tree is
more adapted to the purpose of landscape
than the oak, and that whether singly or
in combination.   In park scenery, a grove
of oaks that have had room to spread,
affords the grandest masses of light and
shadow : and a single oak, whether in full
vigour, or in a state of decay, is ever a
noble and striking object.   The elm, of
which there are several varieties (strikingly different from each other), is a noble
and stately tree, though its character is

less strongly marked, or, if I may be allowed to use the expression, is less hard-featured than the oak or the chesnut. The common elm (the commonest tree in the vicinity of London), when allowed to grow in its natural form, is ample and spreading, as well as lofty. The stem is straighter and more perpendicular than the oak or chesnut; its ramification, not characterized by any strongly marked angles, terminates, when the tree is old and thriving, in large assemblages of sprays, drooping in easy sweeps, as borne downwards by their own weight, but not weeping. Its foliage is rough, entirely devoid of gloss, and so minute as to be expressed by the most shapeless touches; its bark is rough, but so much subdivided as to produce no characteristic effect, except when a wen-like excrescence, bristled over with

minute twigs, forces itself upon the spectator's observation. This tree has the peculiar quality of exhibiting a fair and
thriving outside, not only of trunk and
bark, but of branches, sprays, and foliage,
when its heart is decayed and gone. It
frequently happens that the gale which
oversets it, exhibits to the amazed spectator, a hollow crumbling tube, where he
thought to find a solid and vigorous stem.
Except, therefore, a hole in the trunk,
with the bark curling into it, the elm
should exhibit no marks of decay; nor
ever be presented as stag-headed, except
in the most deplorable state of ruin. Of
a young elm, the characteristics are a
feathery foliage and ramification, and a
disposition to thrive when most excessively
crowded : no tree will bear with truth
being represented as so close planted as
the elm, without appearing to suffer from

it.   Three diameters of the stem will be a
a possible and probable interval.   The
beech is a tree of a very marked and peculiar character ; it is all smoothness, brilliancy, and cheerfulness.   Its trunk, its
ramification, the reverse of the wych
elm, long, slender, and falling easily from
the stem, is concave on the upper side,
the branches and spray turning gently upwards.   Its bark, in all stages of its growth,
is smooth, silvery, and free from moss, exhibiting no furrows but such as arise from
the luxuriance of growth having split the
bark ; its branches are slender, the growth
of its spray invariably pointed, so that it
never becomes clump-headed, and its
whole character is that of perpetual youth.
It may grow huge, it may grow clumsy ;
its stem, in extreme age, may become
thick in comparison to its height, and its

limbs proportionably large and bulky ; its
roots may rise out of the ground and swell
into immense spurs and fantastic knobs ;
but no wrinkles, no dark or rugged appearances on its surface, none of those
symptoms which characterize age or decrepitude in other trees, ever appear on the
beech. It is feathered down to the ground;
its foliage forms into ample masses, with
delicate and pointed terminations, falling
in shelves over each other, which produce
deep shadows and bold lights, that run in
a direction nearly horizontal.

The ash is a tree very different from
any already mentioned. Its general
character is cheerfulness; its growth is
upright; its ramification falls into easy
but decided sweeps, not unlike the
branches of a lustre, rising from the
stem, then depending, and then turning up towards the extremities. The

stem of a very young ash, and the growth
of ash copse, approach nearly to straight
shoots, and never are perfectly straight.
The sprays come off from the stem in
pairs; and each successive pair is nearly
at right angles with the former one.

The bark of a young ash is of a pale
greenish tint; of a full-grown ash, grey,
with spots of whitish moss, and much
subdivided with small furrows running into
each other. The foliage of a young ash is
light and airy; that of a full-grown ash,
sometimes, though not often, luxuriant and
massy. Its autumnal tint is a pale yellow,
harmonizing uncommonly well with the
stronger tints of the fading oak and beech.

The fir tribe have a peculiarity of character, which, at the first glance, distinguishes
them from all other trees. They are in
general unaccommodating in their forms

to picturesque effect, especially when
groups or woods of the same species occur;
and in nature they are seldom combined
with the deciduous tribes. The spruce
and the silver fir, are, in their general
appearance, pyramidical and formal; yet,
when full grown, they sometimes, by
accidental circumstances, become picturesque, especially the spruce.

The larch has not yet been long enough
naturalized in Britain, for us to form any
judgment on its probable appearance in
old age. Its foliage is of a cheerful green;
its growth remarkably rapid and spiry; its
spray long, slender, and flexible in the
extreme. Though a hardy tree, and a
native of the most lofty Alps, where no
other will grow, it is remarkable for
shrinking from the wind; if planted in an
exposed situation, it not only leans from
the most prevalent blast, from its top

down to its very root, but its branches on the windward side even turn round, and point the other way. Its stem, while young, and even when pretty well grown, is remarkable for being thick at the root, and tapering rapidly as it mounts.

In thus speaking of trees, I have confined my observations to some of the principal kinds, most frequent, most useful, and most beautiful in landscape scenery; because, were I to proceed in discriminating all the classes, I should, perhaps, fatigue your attention. There are some remarks, however, applying generally to trees, as materials in landscape pictures, which it will be well to fix in your minds. Trees when young, and consequently thin of foliage, should very rarely be introduced against any part of the landscape as their back ground; they should generally, if introduced at all, be brought to spread their elegant, detailed leafage on the sky, for the purpose of dispersing the solid masses of other trees which have arrived at a state of maturity. When the sun light comes to the spectator, evidently passing through the thinner branches of trees, they will yet be darker than the sky, if opposed to its clear expanse; but if opposed to the landscape, they will, in such case, be lighter than any part of it. In the first of these particulars, Claude Lorraine has shewn the most judicious management and attention ; in the latter, though so great a source of beauty, I do not know of his having made a single experiment. It should be observed and remembered of trees, though landscape-painters seem not to have remembered it, that all trees, favourably planted, will, when full grown, spread their lower branch

to the ground, and even on the ground ;
yet, if supposed in situations to which
cattle of any kind have access, the foliage
will then appear regularly cropped as high
as such cattle can reach.

My remarks on soil, or bare earth, the
next component part of landscape, will be
but few. Soil belongs almost exclusively
to the fore-ground ; and even there, except in the case of a spacious road, a hollow
lane, or a crumbling bank, it will usually
be a very subordinate ingredient. Form
has little to do with it ; tints of various
kinds represent it, and these must be ascertained by the eye. When broken ground
is introduced, as in a gravel pit, quarry,
or crumbling bank, a layer of vegetable
mould, differing in tint from the substra-
tum, usually of a darker colour, and of a
thickness nearly equal throughout, must

be introduced immediately below the turf, or vegetation, whatever it be.

Where a crumbling bank is introduced, the slope at the bottom must be tolerably uniform ; its tints must consist chiefly of those of the upright or overhanging ground, from which its component parts have fallen down.

Where stagnant or smooth water is introduced very near the fore-ground, in contact with bare soil, the soil round the water, imbibing the moisture, will exhibit a narrow border, darker than the dry-ground ; and the flatter the surface of the soil is, the broader this darker margin will be.

In the case of roads, though made roads may differ in tint from the adjoining soil, yet mere footpaths ought not to do so. In many instances, roads partake of the tint of the articles of traffick, for which they are chiefly used. A road in the neighbourhood of a coal pit, or where a coal engine is introduced into the landscape, must be very black; near a lime kiln, whitish; and so of others.

Hills and rocks are the next component parts of landscape. Mountains and hills, of any considerable magnitude, can only find place, as entire objects, in the most remote or in the middle distance; near the eye, parts only, and in the foreground, very small parts of them, can be introduced. However unfettered by rules the forms of rocks may appear to superficial observers, the different species of rocks not only have very separate and distinguishable characters, but they communicate a peculiarity of character to the hills and mountains which they compose.

For this reason, as many beautiful landscapes may be produced without the aid
of rocks, I should humbly advise those,
who have had few opportunities of studying them from nature, not to attempt introducing them into their compositions.
The most obvious division of rocks, for
the purpose of painting, is into those
which are stratified, and those which are
not. The hills formed of the first, are
usually less abrupt and rugged than those
of the other sorts; they frequently lie in
long ridges, forming easy swells; and if
an abrupt break is found in such a hill,
it is usually of a considerable length.
Rocks of this sort are most frequently seen
in the beds and abrupt banks of mountain
streams; where they are found in the greatest abundance, producing the most beautiful effects. It might be supposed that stone

lying in regular layers, would be unpictu-
resque; but that is not the case, the difference of thickness, in the various strata,
their transverse fissures, sometimes very
large and filled with soil, producing luxuriant and ornamental vegetation ; the angular forms into which those fissures break
them, and the bold projecting masses of
superior strata, when the inferior have
been torn away; all these circumstances
contribute to render them more picturesque than almost any species of rock.
If the direction of the stratum points
nearly against the direction of the stream,
and is in itself inconsiderable, small low
cascades are formed, of that sort which
Claude has so happily introduced in his
sweetest compositions, where the water
seems to fall with little disturbance over
broken steps; above those cascades, are

smooth, shallow and transparent pools : if
the dip of the stratum is more rapid, the
pools are deep and dark, and the edges of
the fractured rock, crowding up to-day
from beneath each other, break the water
into irregular, rough and foaming falls.
Rocks of this kind are of various tints,
generally light grey or brown; rarely dark,
and when dark usually bluish, though frequently stained with ochre. Like all other
rocks, when exposed to the air, they collect patches of greenish moss, in such
quantities as to alter their natural tint ;
this, then, in such scenery as I have endeavoured to describe, must be attended
to, the presence or absence of such mosses
marking the greatest height to which the
water usually rises.

    Rocks of granite are in general more
remarkable for the immense bulk of their

masses, than for any thing in their form which renders them peculiarly fit for the pencil. There is another species of rock which I shall mention, on account of its singularity. It is not frequently met with, but is sometimes wonderfully beautiful. I mean that which is gradually formed by water oozing out of the side of a steep and highly stratified bank, and leaving a deposit of limestone. Nothing can be more varied or fantastic than its forms: the icicles of a waterfall are not more so. Porous masses, ramifications like coral, pillars, caverns and cavities, are its usual appearances, with water almost invariably filtering through it in little streamlets, and the most luxuriant vegetation. But at a distance it has little or no effect; it is fit for the foreground only, and there its details will exhaust the utmost skill of the pencil, and perhaps the patience of the artist.

The beauty and interesting appearance of water in landscape, is universally felt and acknowledged, both when real and when expressed by the pencil. In the former instance, it suggests an idea of freshness and fertility; and it seems to animate the view by its motion. In picture, however, considering it as a component part of landscape, I am apt to believe, that some of its beauties arise from a different cause when judiciously introduced. When perfectly tranquil, its smooth glassy surface relieves the eye, by forming a contrast with the many broken and irregular shapes that surround it; and, by reflecting the sky, it serves to interchange and mix the colours of the sky

17

and of the landscape, which would otherwise be two distinct parts of the picture,
uniting only at the extreme distance; a
defect which, without this aid, could only
be obviated by the coloured drapery of
figures, or other extraneous objects inserted for that purpose. Water, when
smooth, and having none but its progressive motion, reflects the surrounding objects, both near and distant; liable to
certain laws of incidence; but if a light
breeze disturb and break the unity of the
surface, then nothing is reflected but the
general colour of the sky. It must also
be fixed, as an indispensable principle, in
your minds, that the reflections in water
are liable, according to its degrees of transparency, to the same laws that influence
the effects of atmosphere in distant ob-

x

jects; it makes the darks lighter, and the lights darker; though this is scarcely perceptible, if the water be perfectly clear.

Of the rules for giving correctly the reflections of objects in water, as a matter of perspective demonstration, I need not speak; because you will hear them ingenuously discussed, in this season, by your lecturer on that branch of art.

The treatment of skies in landscape pictures is important, and its successful result so necessary to the real interest of the whole, that I feel it my duty to make some remarks on the subject. If your practice be in oil-colours, you will *begin* by painting in the blue of the sky, and will afterwards insert the clouds upon that colour, if they be loose and in small detached proportions: if large masses of cloud be intended, then the principal part of the space they are meant to occupy, should be left untouched by the blue. But in both cases the blue must be made gradually lighter as it tends towards the horizon; because the darkness of infinite space is seen through a much greater proportion of enlightened and dense atmosphere in a direction nearly horizontal, than at an) considerable degree of elevation.*

The shadowed parts of the clouds mus next be inserted, making them more an(more blue as they approach the distance and their light parts will follow to be ex ecuted with the purest white that oil ·wil

* For the same reason, it will be obvious, tha mountains and other lofty objects will have their darl colours and shadows darker at and near the summit: than towards the bases. See this point, and other connected with it, illustrated in the Trattato dell. Pittura of da Vinci.

allow, if the sky be to represent a windy, or clear mid-day. If your subject require to suppose the sun low in the picture, as in morning or evening, a new consideration will arise. When the sun's light passes through a dense part of the atmosphere, it will appear discoloured in degrees from *yellow* to red, according to the nature of the medium, and its density ; and will give to all objects on which it falls the kind of colour which it has received in its passage. Thus the colour of the evening light will incline to red, because the gross vapours which have been raised into the sky during the day, begin to descend as the sun retires: thus the colour of the morning light will be yellow, because all the grosser particles have subsided during the night, and the vapour through which the sun's rays then travel is little more than the

pellucid exhalations of the morning dew.
This effect of morning or evening in the
clear expanse of the sky, is exceedingly
difficult to execute in oil-colours. I believe
it is almost impossible to express it truly
in that process. For when the blue has
been regularly diminished, as the truth of
nature requires, from the zenith towards
the horizon, the yellow or red must be
painted in, diminishing also from the horizon till it meet the blue, where the two
colours, naturally so opposite, must be
rubbed or mixed together by means of a
clean brush, and will inevitably produce
a dirty colour, not any thing like that
which in real sky is so beautiful an intermediate between the positive blue and
the positive yellow or red. The contrivance by which painters in oils endeavour to conceal this defect in the nature

of their materials, is by putting some
patches of floating cloud across that part
of the sky where the colours are blended.
But in water-colour painting, this difficulty
does not exist: for the colours are washed
one over the other, and the most perfect
clearness and brilliancy are the consequence. In this latter process there is
also a very simple way of producing the
effect of morning or evening light on the
landscape. When the outline of the subject has been perfected, the whole picture
or drawing must be washed over with a
mixture of Venetian red and gambouge,
inclining more to the first for the evening,
and to the latter for the morning. The
blue expanse of the sky will then be inserted faintly with Prussian blue and as
much carmine as will neutralize the degree of yellowness in the general covering.

The Prussian blue alone will afterwards be employed in recovering the open sky. When this has been duly accomplished, the extreme red or yellow of the sky near the horizon must be given with the same mixture that was used for the general covering, and passed also over all the enlightened surfaces of the landscape. The shadows next, and then the local colours being inserted, the result will be a true appearance of nature under such circumstances.

Having thus had the honour to lead you through a variety of landscape scenery, over mountains, lakes, and rivers, I have no doubt you will be glad of some repose.

LECTURE VI.

Portrait painting is that practice of the art which applies itself to the most pleasing modes of representing truly the persons and features of individuals. I have ever considered this branch of art as one of the painter's indispensable duties; but it has been severely reprobated, by some writers of the last century, as mean and

mercenary to practise it, as vain and frivo-
lous to countenance it ; and, in our own
days, it has been censured in much stronger
terms, even by one of its most successful
practitioners. You will permit me, therefore, to examine the value of portrait
painting, before I attempt to state the
rules and considerations which ought to
guide its proceedings.

It has been stated to us that the first
step towards this kind of personal representation took place in the circumstance
of a faithful lover, when about to lose the
society of his fair mistress, attempting to
draw on a wall the shadow of her features,
which a torch in the room had accidentally
shown him. Thus, then, the practice of
portrait painting had its origin from love.
Can any parentage be more amiable ? Can
the offspring be mean and sordid ? This,

however, it may be said, is poetical fable,
and I can grant that possibly it is so ; but
we will look at facts, and at the arguments
used against portrait painting. It is first
stated to be a very inferior branch of art,
requiring less powers of mind than many
other branches, and, therefore, injurious
to any man of talent who applies himself
to it. This would hold some appearance
of truth with regard to the *practice* two
or more centuries ago, when, generally
speaking, little more was done than painting a head or figure in full light against a
dark back ground ; but, thanks to the per-
severance of Sir Joshua Reynolds, who possessed more taste for colours, and a better
perception of grace than any of his *native*
predecessors, a new style of arranging and
embellishing portrait pictures has been introduced and improved amongst us, which

requires all the manual skill, and a great
part of the theoretical knowledge, of a
consummate artist to make it successful.
In this department of the art, I may say
without hesitation, that the British school
of painting stands higher, in point of excellence, than any school which has preceded it. But it is insisted by those
amongst us, who are ever labouring to
reform human nature into something it
was never meant to be, that the energies
of an art so sublime as painting should
be constantly employed in combinations
which record the deeds of demigods,
heroes, and statesmen, the triumphs of suffering virtue, the punishments of tyranny
and vice, instead of seeking for wealth in
gratifying the vanity of thoughtless individuals. Shall we then, to please these
visionaries, deny to the parting soldier,

who goes to make long and distant war
for his country's interest and glory, the
almost speaking likeness of his weeping
wife, which may cheer his heart in absence and keep it faithful?   Shall the
duteous child no longer look up with reverence to the likeness of a departed parent, hear his virtues recorded, and try to
imitate them?   Every pulse of the feeling heart will, I am convinced, vibrate a
negative to the ridiculous proposal.   The
art of painting was designed to enlighten,
to charm, to soothe the mind and heart,
and it is by the perfection of its energies
in portraiture that some of these most important purposes are successfully accomplished.   I have seen a family of affectionate children come to a portrait painter,
on whose talent they could rely, asking
his assistance to give them a resemblance

of their declining mother, who at last had
yielded to their intreaties for the purpose:
I have seen those children finding conso-
lation, and even joy, in the contemplation
of such a resemblance, after the original
had been taken from them.   Can it be
called degrading to the practices of painting that it has been employed in affording
such alleviations?   Or if a painter be required, as I have more than once experienced, by a distracted mother, to give
her a portrait of the dear daughter, whom
she is on the point of consigning to the
dark chambers of the grave, shall these
high-minded philosophers be allowed to
say that he has administered to vanity,
that he has sought, with the flatteries of
his art, to " soothe the dull cold ear of
death ?" But we will take a wider view of
the subject.   Society is held together by

the most delicate and finely-drawn threads,
beginning with affectionate attachments to
our parents and relations, and extending,
through a variety of minute modifications,
till they include the person of the sovereign who governs us, though perhaps we
may never have seen him.   All this is observable in many countries to a certain
degree ; but in Britain it is obvious to
every one, for every one feels it.   The
branch of painting which we are to consider this morning, unquestionably tends
to promote these feelings, to strengthen
and continue these threads of connection.
The various employments and pursuits of
mankind produce, of necessity, the most
painful, and oftentimes protracted separ-
ations.   The daughter may be called away
from the paternal roof, where she has been
long and fondly cherished, to perform the

14

important duties of a wife and a mother in some far distant region. The son may be compelled, in spite of the danger of feverish climates, to make perilous voyages for the advancement of that commerce which is the glory and strength of our nation ; and both son and father, enthusiasts in the defence of their country, may be suddenly required,·in distant plains, to assert its proud pre-eminence. In such cases as these, where the heart throbs with anguish that the judgment cannot restrain, the pencil of the portrait painter affords the only probable mitigation. The dear resemblance, in each case, is held close to the bosom as a treasure: the parent thinks he has lost but half his enjoyment, and the distant child, looking frequently on the venerated image which he possesses, feels a new incitement to the practice of those virtues which he had learnt from paternal example.   But if portraits can thus become the means of soothing that tender and delicate grief, which arises from temporary separation, how infinitely greater must be their influence when the dear forms are snatched from us for ever! There are many here present, I cannot doubt it, who know this by sad experience; I will not, therefore, urge the argument further.   I may, however, be allowed to add, that it is in anticipation of this painful certainty that we entreat, nay, supplicate, our relations and friends for their resemblances, and generally, I believe, obtain an extorted compliance, in which vanity has no share.   That the multiplied portraits of a beloved monarch have the happiest effects in exciting and in strengthening attachment, may be seen almost in every part of this kingdom, but particularly in the north. I am well acquainted with many houses in those parts, the proprietors of which have never seen our present sovereign, and yet where some kind of painting or engraving of him is preserved with as much care as the ancients bestowed on their household deities. In the representation of those public events which contribute to secure our national greatness, and to extend our military and naval glory, we look anxiously for the faithful portraits of the heroes who achieved them. It is a tribute of public gratitude that must be more soothing to the illustrious objects of it, than the wealth or titles so justly bestowed.

Taking portrait painting, then, as a great and essential branch of the art, we will proceed to consider some of the rules and principles by which its practices should be governed. The true object of painting is to imitate nature, and in no department of the art is it more evidently required to be so, than in the one before us. Perfect resemblance to the natural object, constitutes, oftentimes, the entire value of such performances, and it ought to be striking and unequivocal at first sight, or the artist has not done his duty. This, too, is an excellence in art of which any person is able to judge, though wholly ignorant of the intricate means by which the back grounds and effects of such pictures are combined and brought together. Yet, even here, we find that attempts have been made, and are still making, to introduce that abstract or general representation, as it is called, which I have had occasion to speak of in a former Lecture, as so prejudicial to the true

style of painting. The professed object,
on such occasions, is to conceal every appearance of individual marking, on the
face to be represented. Some have endeavoured to accomplish it by broad and extensive shadows; some have tried, for the
same purpose, broad lights, almost without any shadows; and others have had
recourse to an artifice, less justifiable, in
spreading a muslin or thin veil over their
window, that every part of the object
might be undefined and tender, as they
call it, by not being distinctly seen; but
all these three sorts have invariably con-
curred in rejecting every appearance of a
dark shadow, in or about the face, except
one under the nose. These contrivances
can add nothing to the inimitable charms
of youth and beauty; and, in the portraits
of age thus produced, instead of those in-

dications of the progress of time which
are so venerable, and so picturesque, we
often see hollow eyes, sunken cheeks, and
mouths fallen in for want of teeth, with
a skin fair, sleek and blooming. We will
not follow this practice. The first, and
fundamental principle of portrait painting,
as I have stated before, is resemblance;
but it must be a resemblance under the
most favourable circumstances possible to
the subject. These circumstances having
been once assumed, or supposed, the most
correct and faithful imitation of the whole
should necessarily follow. The first rule
that I would wish to give you is, that all
figures for portraits should be placed in a
broad and diffusive light, like that of the
open air, admitted by one window only.
Under these circumstances, the reflected
lights are always strong, and the shadows

never so dark as to be harsh and disagreeable. Besides, it is the kind of light in
which objects are commonly seen and
familiarized to us, and, therefore, to place
them in artificial lights in which they
perhaps never appeared but by the direction of the painter, is to take so much
from the effect of likeness. I will not
trouble you with remarks on the thought-
lessness of those artists who shut up the
light of their painting rooms to about a
foot square, and yet do not hesitate, in
finishing the heads of persons depicted in
this prison-like light, to give them back-
grounds of a clear blue sky, as if they had
not previously scorned the cheering rays
of the sun. I have perfect confidence in
laying down this rule for your guidance,
as I am convinced it will greatly contribute to your success. Rubens, whose

portraits are amongst his finest works, certainly placed his objects in a very open light; his window, if I may credit the assertion of those who have visited and examined his residence, being nearly equal to the whole side of his painting room. Vandyke, the finest portrait painter that ever existed, appears to me to have practised on the same principle.

The next point to which I would direct your attention, is, the position of the head in a portrait, relatively with that of the body. The body and the head should, I think, never be presented in the same direction to the spectator, except in the case of very old persons, where the facility of motion is diminished by a variety of causes, and then I would advise to turn the figure about one-third from the front, and allow the eyes to look on ; that is, at the observer. But in cases of extreme age, even this cannot be allowed without a deviation from propriety of character. It is generally supposed, that a portrait is rendered more interesting when the eyes look on; and, no doubt, the observation has much reason : yet I have seen many instances, in which a great appearance of dignity has been given, by putting the body in front, and turning the head and the eyes so as to look entirely out at the side of the picture. In speaking on this point, I ought not to omit pointing out to you, as a caution, the mistake very commonly made by Sir Godfrey Kneller, and Sir Peter Lely, of putting the body of a figure in front, with the head turned aside, and yet having the eyes looking on. This circumstance is also to be met with in the portraits by Jervois and by Hudson.

In portraits of whole figures, if single, they will generally be represented standing, though recumbent or sitting positions may be admitted for the purpose of favouring some personal defect; but even then the eye of the spectator should be carried up to the top of the picture, by some upright object or other; the stumps of trees are the common, and, I may say, threadbare auxiliaries on such occasions. If more than one figure be required in the picture, they are then, as far as the grouping extends, to be governed by the

rules of composition, which you will find
detailed by many writers on painting;
particularly by Gerrard Lairesse, and by
Hogarth, in his Analysis of Beauty. If the
figure required to be represented, be un-
graceful through excessive bulk, you will
not correct it by paring the form down to
the dimensions of a Niobe, or an Apollo;
thus, as is not unfrequently the case, setting a fat countenance on a slender body;
but you will correct the probable impression of its bulk by accessory objects, art-
fully introduced to conceal part of its
extent. If the figure of the intended
portrait be thinner than is consistent with
the idea of symmetry, the defect, in a female, may be easily concealed, by the
introduction of loose and flowing drapery,
and by covering one arm entirely, and
fore-shortening the other; but if the figure

be that of a man, and you are confined to
the close dress of modern Europe, then
the task is not so easy : you have perhaps
no way left for concealing the defect, but
that so judiciously recommended by Sir
Joshua Reynolds, in his notes to Mason's
translation of Du Fresnoy, the best work,
in my opinion, that ever came from the
pen of that distinguished painter : his advice consists in introducing some object
of the same colour, which you are obliged
to adopt for the drapery, and placing it so
that it may seem, in the general appearance, to be an extension of the figure.　In
finishing this part of my subject, I am very
strongly inclined to say, that I would prefer almost any artifice to a deviation from
truth, which nothing can justify.　In the
back-grounds of your portraits, which, if
small, should be very simple, and, if large,

may perhaps consist of many objects, every
thing should be subordinate to the interest
of the figure ; not by making a midnight
sky behind a head that seems to receive
the meridian sun, or by glazing down the
objects after they have received a correct
light and shadow; but by being chosen
of such tones and materials, as will necessarily answer your purpose, without a
violation of truth.   For this purpose, the
materials offered by nature are ample;
they are inexhaustible, without exposing
you to the risk of wearing out any set
of ideas.   If the back-grounds of your
pictures necessarily consist of distant objects, they should, I think, be indistinct,
and slightly executed; even more so than
the same degree of distance in pictures of
landscape.   For, suppose the whole composition of the picture to be really before

you, the eye, in passing rapidly from a
very near object, the figure, to a very remote distance, does not immediately adapt
its focus to the change of circumstances,
as it would be enabled to do in landscape,
by passing through the intermediate dis-
- tances.   To which may be added, that as
the attention of the spectator is intended
to be fixed on the figure, the focus of the
eye must be supposed to be adjusted to
that precise distance at which the figure
stands; and, consequently, the back-ground
or distance, to which that focus is not
supposed to be adjusted, ought to be more
indistinct.   An attention to this optical
effect gives wonderful relief to the portrait.   Sir Joshua Reynolds seems to have
been fully aware of it, and the back-
grounds of his pictures are oftentimes
inimitably excellent.   On back-grounds, I

18

have only two more remarks to make at present. I must take the liberty of suggesting to you, if they be composed of landscape, not to repeat the common-place distance of a row of formal trees, showing between them the bright shine of a running stream. This device you must have so frequently met with, that it is impossible you should not have been struck with it. I must also beg leave to call your serious attention to the back-grounds of your portraits, with a view to their perspective propriety. The horizontal line for the head of your figure, which most probably you take sitting, should be somewhere between the bottom of the nose and the middle of the throat, and in removing the subject to stand at a distance for the convenience of drawing the whole figure, if a whole length be required,

you must observe that the visual rays
which touched the horizon on your subject at the first station, should, by being
produced, touch exactly the same points
of the person as before, or you will see
the face differently from what you have
represented it, and which is consequently
inconsistent with truth.

The perspective horizon for your back-grounds, must never be placed lower than you observe it in this new station of the figure, which will give it you somewhere about the waist. It cannot be placed lower, without a most flagrant departure from probability and truth; yet we often see, in the landscapes that accompany modern portraits, the horizontal line placed as low as the feet of the figure. All these points, then, being fully weighed and considered, we will suppose the object you intend to paint is seated before you. At this moment you will perceive the difficulty of the task you have undertaken, the importance and value of the branch of art in which you are engaged.

The artist who paints pictures of invention, whether historical or of any other kind, has so many auxiliary aids at com-

mand, by which to furnish out his composition, that a failure in any one can arise
only from want of taste, or from want of
knowledge ; but in the case of portraits,
where the subject is always given, frequently of the most unfavourable kind,
and a fine picture expected, there is, as-
suredly, no one principle of the art,
whether of composition, of light and
shadow, or of colouring, that will not be
indispensable to complete the arduous undertaking.

But having gone through these prepa-
ratory observations, and being on the point
of sitting down to the delightful occupation, for such I must call it, of painting a
portrait, I must remind you that there is,
in every set of features, in every countenance, a variety of changes, each having
its particular power to please, and that the

impression we have of any person's face,
as an acquaintance, arises from the whole
of these taken together.   The portrait
painter, however, can represent, consistently, but one moment of countenance,
but one position of features.   This moment should, therefore, be chosen of the
most pleasing kind, and, once assumed,
every part of the face should partake of
the appropriate expression.   In violation
of this necessary observance, we frequently
see portraits, especially in small, with the
eyes languid, the brows frowning, and yet
the mouths pinched up at the corners
into a simper, lest the face should look
grave.

It next becomes necessary to determine
in what process of painting you will produce the intended resemblance.   The first
that offers itself to our notice, as being at

z

present most general, is that of painting in oils. I have had the honour to prove to you, in a former lecture, that pictures, executed in this process, are not amongst the most permanent ; yet, as it is a practice which many may wish to attempt, because it gives a facility of rudely covering a large space in a short time, and as I would not be suspected of unjust partiality to the mode of painting, which I have advised you to prefer, I shall avail myself of this opportunity to give some remarks on the use and application of oil colours.

The pigments employed in this process are the same as those made use of in water, and they are mixed up in boiled linseed oil, in nut oil, or in poppy oil ; the first for the dark colours, and the other two for the light colours, because they have less tendency to turn yellow by time. That all oils had this tendency to turn yellow, was well known even in the time of Vassari, who has mentioned it in his writings upon the art. Many artists also paint a great deal in a mixture of boiled linseed oil and mastic varnish, which makes the colours dry much sooner than oils alone. It would be difficult to lay down rules for the mode of proceeding, because the use of these colours cannot be reduced to philosophical principles, as may be done with water colours, and because even the best masters have differed materially in their practice. The earliest examples we have of this kind of painting, and which, even now, appear the least discoloured by time, were certainly painted on a white distemper ground, strongly sized with glue; so that the oils could not immediately penetrate, though they

might be absorbed by it to a certain degree afterwards, and thus be prevented
rising to the surface. The outline was
carefully and correctly drawn on this
ground with a small point of chalk; and
the lightest colours laid in first, proceeding
regularly downwards to the darkest. By
this mode of proceeding, which is evident
on examining the oil pictures of Da Vinci
and Raphael, the lightest, or brightest
parts, had least colour on them, and could
not, therefore, undergo so great a change
by the effect of the oils. Other painters
of those times adopted the practice, which
has been partially revived of late, of painting their subjects in with two colours, to
represent the light and shadow, as I had
the honour of recommending to you in the
use of water colours, and then glazed every
object, or part, over with its appropriate

hue, made transparent by means of oils or
varnish.   1 have stated to you before the
reasons why this mode of proceeding
could not succeed with oil colours, unless
in cases of very smooth pencilling.   Rubens, who generally used a white ground,
made his outline very perfect, with some
dark kind of crayon, and then laid in his
shadows with terre de Cassel, rendered
thin with varnish.   To this he added,
on the edges of the shadows, the grey
tints, generally very strong, then the reds,
near the high lights; and having glazed
the whole, excepting the shadows, over
with a semi-transparent flesh colour, he
inserted the brightest or shining light
with solid colour, sometimes projecting to
a degree that is highly objectionable.
Vandyke, the scholar of Rubens, gave a
truer colour to the shadows in his faces,

by rejecting the disagreeable browness of the Cassel earth : he imitated his object more closely than his master ; and I have no doubt we ought to consider him as the best example in portrait painting that the world has produced.

The present practice of portrait painting in oils, is to sketch out the subject very slightly with chalk, and then to correct the outline with a red or brownish colour. To this succeeds a dead colouring, as it is called, consisting of dark tints of red, black, and purple, which are to be neutralized and softened down in the next stage of the process, by semi-transparent tints, inclining to yellow. This mode of practice may, in skilful hands, produce an appearance of truth when fresh from the painter's easel ; but the lamentable consequence is, that in time the dark colours underneath, appear, with increasing force, through the upper covering, and produce an effect wholly incompatible with beauty. The present appearance of almost every portrait painted by Sir Joshua Reynolds, is a complete confirmation of my opinion. I have, therefore, no hesitation in recommending to you Vandyke, as a model in portrait painting; for his process, if you paint in oils, and for his general truth of imitation, if your process be of any other kind. There are many persons, seemingly conversant with pictures, who will advise you to take Titian for your model, and will justify their recommendation on his acknowledged eminence; they will tell you such, or such, is the colouring of this master, and that you should endeavour to copy it; but, in their enthusiasm for foreign painters, they forget that Titian,

who doubtless painted most truly his originals, painted always the dark, yet clear,
complexion of the Italians, which would
ill suit on unsunned English faces.   Vandyke, besides being a complete master in
this branch of art, was invariably employed
in climates nearly like our own ; and his
heads are, therefore, the best we can find
to guide us in our imitation of nature.

   I turn, with great satisfaction, from these
considerations, to the practice of painting
in water colours, which is so superior in
many respects, particularly in its greater
permanency, that I venture to recommend
it to you as the only process of painting
suited to those who paint for amusement
only.

   Your outline being completed with
black lead, minutely describing all the
details of the features, you will proceed

to give the first and second shadows with
Indian ink, as described in my third lee-
ture, frequently repeating those of the
second class, till you get the true undulations of the light surfaces. After this will
follow the grey tints, the general and partial colouring, and last the finishing of the
shadows, as I have explained before. I
am perfectly convinced in my own mind,
that this mode of painting in heads as
large as the natural, is much better calculated for expressing female or infantine
beauty, than any other at present in use.
It may, perhaps, be in my power, at a
future opportunity, to show you some
specimens illustrative of this opinion. At
present, it is my wish rather to engage
your attention to the practice of portrait
painting in miniature, than in any other
mode, and to give you a series of rules

for your guidance. The principles I have
already laid down in this lecture, are applicable to portrait painting of any size,
and in any process ; and, allow me to add,
that to execute a picture well in small,
requires as much reflection and science,
and more manual skill, than to execute
the same subject equally well in large.

The history of miniature painting furnishes examples of three distinct modes of
practice ; in oils, in enamel, and in water
colours. The first of these processes I
have had the honour of showing you, is
unavoidably liable to a very considerable
degradation of the light colours, which,
if evident in large masses, must be fatally
injurious to the delicacy and gradual effect
of small pictures. Besides, the thickness
of the materials, however finely prepared,
precludes the possibility of discriminating

the small parts of the features as they
ought to be discriminated in subjects of
very small dimensions. I cannot, therefore, recommend this mode of miniature
painting to your adoption.   Still less
should I feel inclined to advise the practice of enamelling for those who do not
make a profession of it. It is true we
have many beautiful specimens in this
process of miniature painting, by Pettitoe,
by Zinck, and still better by our country-
man and contemporary, Mr. Bone; but as
the colours, when applied, are of tints
totally different from what they are to appear after the operation of the furnace, it
requires many years of constant and laborious experiment to calculate the possible
and probable change of them, with any
prospect of success. There are, besides
this, other objections to enamel painting,

which bear great weight in my mind ; but
it is not necessary to urge them. The
process of miniature painting, which remains to be examined, and which I mean
to recommend, is that of water colours
on ivory. I have shown you already that
the earliest attempts in this branch, some
of them as far back as the time of our
glorious King Alfred, are painted in water
colours, constantly mixed with white for
the lighter parts of the objects, whether
drapery or flesh. In the performances of
Sir Antonio More, of Hilliard, and of
Oliver, we find a partial abandonment of
this practice ; for the lights in many of
their heads are left of the colour of the
vellum, or distemper ground on which
they painted ; but as they generally exe-
ecuted the other parts of their pictures in
body or distemper colours, and as gene-

rally shaded every colour with a darker
tint of the same kind, there is in them a
distinctness, a separation of all the parts,
which hurts the eye, because it is never
to be found in nature. The use of body
colours, in miniature painting, was, however, gradually relinquished in this country; and, forty years ago, they were
scarcely admitted, I believe, except for
backgrounds, where least of all they ought
to be suffered. I am inclined to think,
though I am not certain, that the late
Mr. Myers was the first who performed
miniature pictures entirely with transparent colours. At what time ivory was
first resorted to as a surface to paint on,
I cannot ascertain ; it was probably not
further back than the beginning of the
last century; but of this I have no doubt,
that it is, when properly prepared, the best

ground for the purpose that has yet been attempted or employed. You will take first a mixture of carmine, gamboge, and Indian ink *, differently proportioned according to the complexion of the subject, and make a correct outline, beginning with the eye-lashes, if both eyes are visible, or with the top of the forehead, if a side face. If you find these lines correct in the direction, and in the distance from each other, you will immediately draw the dark shape of the nostrils, comparing their situation with a supposed perpendicular line from the inner corner of each eye, and also with a supposed diagonal line

* The portions of the red and the yellow represent the local, or flesh, colour; and the Indian ink gives the portion of black, which constitutes the degree of shadow. See this principle explained and exemplified, in a former lecture.

from the outer corner of each eye to the point between the nostrils, by which means you will get the place of the nose correct. In the same way you will get the middle line of the mouth, and a line for the edge of the chin. This being done, one great difficulty is surmounted; and you will continue, with the same mixture, to delineate the detail of the features; in doing which, no particular should be omitted, but the upper line of the under eye-lid. If this be done with truth, the resemblance is certain, and the remainder of the work rather delightful than laborious. I must beg leave here to repeat, that likeness, in portrait painting of every kind, depends on making a perfect outline at first.

Your next step will be, with the same

three colours, to express the shadows of
the first class, adding rather more of the
carmine in those parts where the light,
passing through the thin texture of some
of the features, imbibes a portion of the
colour. But we must here stop to consider, that, as the ivory does not absorb
the colours we employ, so far differing
from paper, which has considerable power
of absorption, we cannot spread them
smooth in large breadths on the bare surface of ivory or over each other. Thus
we are obliged to have recourse to stip-
pling or hatching, of which the latter is
unquestionably the best. You will also
find it necessary to use, with your colours,
a solution of two-thirds fine gum-arabic,
and one-third white sugar candy, so as to
attach the first covering of colour to the

14

ivory very strongly. In subsequently going over, less of this vehicle may be used; because, if the first coat of colours have a sufficient quantity of it, the moisture of those that follow will partly dissolve the first gum, and incorporate them with it. You will also keep at hand some double distilled vinegar, to dilute the colour when it becomes thick in the pencil; it decomposes the gum for a time, and renders the colour more limpid than it would be with the same portion of common, or even of distilled water. You will observe, in regard to the texture of your colours, that they must be so moist as to part immediately from the pencil, and yet so thick by their substance, or by the gum, as not to leave an accumulation, or little spot, at the end of each line. In expressing your first shadow, if the portions be

A A

small, or long and narrow, the direction of
the lines or hatches must be in the direction of the part to be expressed. If the
shadows are broad, you will take the direction of the lines diagonally from the left
at the bottom, to the right at the top;
observing, invariably, that the lines be of
the same thickness all along, at no time
ending in points, and, also, that the distance between them be so precisely regular and equal, that a second course of
lines, given upon the intervals, may touch
the first lines on each side all the way,
and thus produce a flat colour. You will
next insert the blue and grey tints, with
ultra-marine, or ultra-marine and vermilion: those that appear at the edges of
the first shadows must be inserted in
places left for them between the first
course of lines, and those that are local

must be expressed in lines parallel to the direction of the part on which they appear. The red colours, or reddish tints, will be the next object of your attention, which you will invariably express with different mixtures of carmine and vermilion. This brings the head to what ought to be accomplished at the first sitting, and which, when you are familiarized to the practice, will require nearly an hour and a quarter. The next stage, or sitting of your picture, should be to give the general colour with carmine and gamboge, or with Venetian red and gamboge, covering the whole face, except the highest lights, darker or lighter, according to the complexion to be expressed. The course of lines, in this operation, should be diagonally, from left to right, and the intervals between should be exactly equal

to the breadth of the lines, that, by repeating the operation, the intervals may
be precisely filled up to a perfectly even
colour. The variations of the local colours
must then be given, in lines obliquely
crossing those that appear from the first
sitting, and the colours of the reflected
lights must be inserted in the same manner. The hair should afterwards be drawn,
and shadowed with a broad pencil, and
the figure delineated. The colour of the
iris of the eyes, if dark, will be expressed
with the hair and eye-brows, or if blue,
or grey, at the time of giving those tints
in the first sitting. The interval which
you will now take, previous to the third
and last view of your object, should be
employed in painting the back-ground,
and in shadowing and colouring the
drapery. The tint, or kind of colour,

which you adopt for the ground behind your heads, is a point for serious deliberation. If your subject be 'pale, you will endeavour to give it warmth by contrasting it with the ground; if the complexion have an excess of brown or red, you will contrive to incline the ground to those colours by which the excess will be apparently diminished. But in your first experiments I would advise you, by all means, to paint your heads on a bright blue sky ground; for when you can produce one that will bear this comparison, without looking dirty, you will be equal to the most beautiful and delicate effects on any other ground. But the mode of executing a back-ground, especially if required to appear flat, is not easy, without much practice. The general colour, whatever it be, must be washed over, diluted with a strong mixture of the gum, for the reasons stated before; and when that is dry, the lighter parts, where a less proportion of colour has remained, must be filled up with lines, in the direction of the part, being neither small nor close together, so that, at a short distance, the general colour may appear equal. The whole must then be worked over in short and rather thick lines, smaller than before, in any direction; observing only that the lines must be neater near the head, and that the intervals between the lines and touches of the back-ground must invariably be equal to the thickness of the lines or touches. These observations will likewise apply to the painting of any dark draperies, and also to the shadows of those that are white. I must, however, beg leave to caution you against the very general practice, amongst miniature painters, of making the shadows of white draperies brown; the folly and impossibility of which I have shown in a former Lecture. If the proper effect of the picture require buff colour, or brown, in such parts, it would surely be more worthy the talent of an artist to insert there some additional drapery of that hue, than to violate the unerring laws of Nature. In the last sitting you take of your object, your first operation will be to express the shadows of the second class with a mixture of the local colour of the part, and the three colours composed as you used them for the first shadows. Then will follow the shadows of the third and fourth classes, with the same materials, observing to mix more carmine, or even carmine and vermilion, in some of the darkest touches about the eyes, the nose, and the mouth, or, perhaps, the ear a little, but never under the chin. I ought to have observed to you, that the brightest specks on the eyes should be left of the clear ivory, at the time when the pupils are inserted with the three colours at the first sitting. After the finishing of the last shadows, as I have just described, the white speck must be given exactly on the place left for it. Thus the face of your miniature will be completely finished in a time, not exceeding four hours in all, and the hair, background, and drapery, may perhaps occupy you, from first to last, about six hours more.

Having now carried you through the complete execution of a miniature picture, in a way that you will find easy, certain, and delightful, my further remarks will apply to the practice in any process. It has been supposed by many, that the painting of likenesses is a kind of gift, or inherent talent, not universally possessed by artists, and this idea has been industriously propagated by many. Whether it has been so propagated by such as have failed, for the purpose of extenuating their want of exertion, and consequent failure, or by those who have been successful, to excite veneration for their talents, is of little importance at present; but that the supposition is wholly unfounded, I have no hesitation in asserting. The most complete success in any kind of portrait painting is within every one's reach, if he set out on right principles, and any less degree of success will unquestionably be in proportion to his ardour and his assiduity.

In regard to the particular mode which we have just been discussing, I have to remark to you, that an opinion has prevailed with some artists, that miniature pictures should represent their objects, as seen at that degree of distance which would reduce them to the same angle which the picture subtends with the eye, when seen at a proper distance, and should, therefore, show in their shadows and darks, that grey, or, as some have made it, purple, which is the effect of atmosphere. I cannot but look on this opinion as erroneous; for if objects were removed so far from us as to be liable to this alteration of their appearance by the intervening atmosphere, the parts on which the resemblance depends would not be discernible at all. I am rather inclined to think that miniature pictures should represent their objects as they would appear through a diminishing glass, when all the parts, tones, and colours, are retained, though reduced to a less extent.

Having thus examined the principles and the practice of portrait painting, the difficulties that attend its execution, and the benefits it confers on society, you will, I trust, concur with me in allowing that it is an important branch of the painter's profession, and that it should ever be considered as one of the finest sources of sentimental enjoyment.

LECTURE VII.

I HAVE already shown you the great importance of engraving in promoting national objects. I have already shown you its wide extended utility in publishing and in diffusing almost every kind of knowledge in art and science. I have endeavoured, also, to impress upon your minds, from those demonstrations, the necessity you are under, as a public duty, to patronise the art of engraving with all the proper means in your power. But to patronise any art effectually, you must understand its means, its object, and its pretensions; and therefore, with a view to that important end, I purpose devoting this morning's Lecture to that discussion only.

In the early periods of engraving it was an art of the most simple operation, consisting of nothing more than cutting with a tool; but the ingenuity of succeeding times has multiplied its materials, its implement and its modes of proceeding, and hence have arisen much argument, much serious disputation, both public and private; as to which mode is the best. We will enter on the examination of this question in its proper place, and in doing so we will not take for our guide the dictum of any professor in the art, because we know how natural it is in every man to stickle for the supposed superiority of his own practice. We will for this purpose establish a set of well-founded principles for our standard, and then bring the different modes of engraving to it, like recruits for measurement, and see which will best pass the muster.

Engraving is that art of imitating natural objects, the result of which is to be transferred to paper, or some other material, by means of pressure. It is performed by incision or by corrosion, and the medium of transfer is delivered sometimes from the cavities, and sometimes from the remaining surface. But this art of imitating natural objects is carried on invariably by the intervention of drawing or painting. The engraver cannot take his copper into the woods and fields, and impress upon it with his instruments the scene that appears before him; he cannot

13

by means of his art singly, delineate and
shadow the face and person of his friend
or of his employer; he cannot take the
glowing ideas of the poet or the historian,
and embody them at once on his cold
material. Thus then the engraver, whose
proper object is to do that in black which
the painter has already accomplished in
colours, may be considered as the painter's shadow: he follows him every where,
keeps close to him, and cannot exist without him. It is true many engravers have
been, who engraved their own compositions; but in doing this they only united
the character and occupation of painter
to the duties of their first profession, and
such instances therefore do not in the
least disprove the complete dependence
of engraving on the sister arts. Engraving, properly so called, is the art of mak-

ing incisions with an edged and pointed instrument, to represent the forms and shadows of objects. Where, when, or by whom this art was first practised is very uncertain, as I had the honour of stating to you in my first Lecture. Vasari gives the merit of the invention to his own country, while others, with great appearance of probability, suppose it to have taken place in Germany or Flanders, somewhat earlier; but it is an evident fact that we have examples of engraving, where shadows are expressed by lines, and even by cross lines, nearly two centuries before the time fixed for the supposed discovery: these examples are to be found in the brass tablets let into some of the grave-stones occasionally found in the ailes of some of our oldest churches. It is probable, however, that the practice of engraving such tablets existed long before any attempt was made to take impressions from them. It is also worthy of remark, that the earliest impression we have of any kind of engraved plate, appears to have been taken with a clearness and precision that show the copper-plate printer's art not to be then in its infancy.

Engraving, for the purpose of printing, has almost invariably been executed on plates of copper, brought to a fine, firm, and equal texture by careful and long continued hammering on the anvil. The plates are then rubbed steadily for a length of time with a large piece of strong charcoal dipped in water, to take out the marks of the hammer, and are afterwards again rubbed with a finer charcoal soaked in oil to give them a polish ready for the artist: the preparation of the plate is the same for every mode of engraving. The copper produced in this island, either from its peculiar quality, or from the superior manner in which it is manufactured by our coppersmiths, has long been considered as the best; and, till the ambition of an insatiable conqueror led him to think of setting bounds to British commerce, the engravers of the continent had the chief part of their plates from London.

The plate being ready to receive the subject, a considerable difficulty occurred to the early engravers as to the means of transferring it to the copper with accuracy: it was, however, generally performed thus. The plate was rubbed very thinly over with white wax, and a tracing of the subject having been made on thin paper with some kind of crayon, the

drawing was laid with its face to the wax,
and by rubbing gently on the back of the
paper was soon transferred and reversed.
A pointed instrument was then used to
trace through the wax on the lines so
transferred, and to scratch the subject
faintly into the copper, after which the
wax was cleared away and the ártist left
at liberty to proceed. The great difficulty of deciding the direction in which
the lines should be laid on the different
objects, was obviated by many of the
early engravers, who, with a degree of
patience that is now almost incredible,
made drawings with a pen to work from,
in which they inserted every line that was
to be afterwards introduced in their plates.
The implements for this species of art
are five or six engravers of various lengths
and thicknesses, as many points of various

sizes; a scraper, a burnisher, and an oil-
rubber: to these the engravers of modern
times have added an anvil, a hammer, and
a pair of calipers, by which they are enabled to beat out and repair any part of
the work that may seem to be ill done;
a convenience which in these times seems
very much resorted to. The great clearness which a dextrous engraver can give
to his lines by his steadiness in cutting
them, is his highest praise as a mechanic;
but the manner of distributing and dis-
posing those lines, as well as of deciding
their various thicknesses, is a subject that
requires much science, long practice and
deep thought, without which little hope
can be entertained of ever arriving at
excellence in this art. Indeed the difficulty is so great, that out of the vast
numbers who have attempted it, not
above one in a hundred has ever estab-

lished claims to be considered as any thing better than a mere mechanic. It will, doubtless, readily occur to you in considering this art, that the steadiness and force required in urging the tool forwards in a given direction must greatly abridge the freedom of execution, and render it almost impossible adequately to express, by such means, the appearance of rough or uneven surfaces, the light and playful foliage of trees, or the thin floating vapours of the atmosphere. You will perceive the nature and extent of this difficulty to the 'graver*, on looking at the landscapes in the plates of Albert Durer, of Martin Schon; and particularly in those of Sadlaer after Brughel and Paul Bril. The early engravers endeavoured, though ineffectually, to remove this difficulty, by

* Technical, for the instrument employed.

working with their plate on a sand-bag, or hard cushion, by which they were enabled to turn the plate about with the left hand to meet the point of the tool which was sometimes held firm and sometimes pressed forwards with the right. The use of such a cushion has, however, been generally laid aside, since the etching-needle has been employed to do that which was found so incompatible with the nature of the 'graver. The early engravers, as I have had occasion to state to you before, never attempted to express more than the drawing and the actual light and shadow of the pictures they copied, leaving the copper untouched for the lightest part of every object, not placed in shadow, and they seem to have avoided as much as possible the frequent crossing of their lines. Some have endeavoured to accomplish their works with single lines only, as we see particularly in the works of Melan, but the appearance is generally without force, and has more claim to be looked on as an affectation than as a merit.

Engraving on wood was probably cotemporary with engraving in plates of metal; but the first specimens of this kind which have reached us, deserving of notice, are in the works of Albert Durer. These are scarce, and consequently valuable; and it is usual to call them very fine, which they unquestionably are, both in composition and drawing, perhaps also in expression; but we must not let these properties, which belong to them as pictures, delude our judgments when considering them as engravings. If a great literary character were to write an elegant, and perspicuous

dissertation on the beauties of Christianity,
and were to write it with the point of a
skewer, we should not call the hand-writ-
ing beautiful, because the language glowed
with celestial enthusiasm. ·It is on this
principle that we must look at the set of
scripture subjects, engraved on wood by
Durer, which, in point of mechanical excellence, are as much inferior to the engravings in wood, produced at this time,
as Perugino was in painting to his illustrious disciple.   Engraving in wood is
executed on a principle different from that
of engraving on copper.   In the latter, the
printing ink is delivered unto the paper
from the cavities made by the artist ; in
the former, the lines intended to receive
and deliver the ink are left standing, and
the remaining surface is cut away. The
early engravers of this kind performed

their works with various sorts of knives,
which you will find described and delineated in an ingenious French work on this
art, by Papillon: the engravers in wood of
the present day, who have carried the practice so much nearer to perfection, make
use of no other than the common engraving tools, with the exception of a large
square tool, called a scawper, with which
they clear out the larger cavities for the
spaces that are to appear white in the impression.   But the mode of engraving on
wood is now entirely different in principle
from what it was before.   At first the
object seems to have been to imitate in
this way the appearance of engravings
on copper, and a very ingenious wood engraver of our own time has done, perhaps,
all that can be done in that way ; but even
supposing it possible to equal the other

art, which, in point of delicacy and softness,
it never can, it must cost much greater
labour to achieve it, and when accomplished, the great boast is no more than that it
is a faithful resemblance of engraving in
copper, which is an imitation of painting,
which is an imitation of nature. This
idea has, therefore, been wisely abandoned,
and the present system of engraving in
wood is to effect the intended appearance
by cutting white lines and touches with
black spaces, instead of giving black lines
or dots with white intervals, as is done on
copper. But the practitioner of this art
has great disadvantages to encounter in
the difficulty he finds of getting his work
printed even tolerably; and critics, not
well informed on the subject, have often
decried as defects, in such productions, the
blackness of many parts which was en-
18

tirely owing to the clumsiness of the printers.

Engraving in mezzotinto was invented by Prince Rupert. He observed one morning a centinel cleaning from the barrel of his musket a rust which the night dew had formed upon it, and fancied, as it became gradually bright in one part after another, that he could trace some kind of figure in the different degrees of brightness and rust. This led to the idea of making the surface of a plate rough by corrosion or other means, and then to form a figure upon it, by polishing it more or less in different parts. When this had been accomplished, the desire to try if it would contain any kind of printing ink would follow of course. This art has claims upon your notice and protection, of a peculiar kind: it is a native of Britain, and has never been practised successfully in any other country.

The plate for this practice is first raked, notched, or punched all over, in different directions, with what is called a grounding tool, till it will yield a perfectly black impression in every part. The plate being thus prepared with a proper ground, the subject must be communicated to it by means of chalking the back of the paper on which it is drawn, which must be laid on the copper, and then the form traced over with a point on the drawing side. The lines which will thus be left of white chalk on the plate, must be drawn again with a black lead pencil, or Indian ink, to make them more permanent. The original black ground is then to be scraped away, and even burnished quite smooth in some parts, to represent the different

tones of the picture to be copied, so that
nothing of the ground in its first state
remains, but where it is intended to express the deepest shadows. The masses
of strongest light are given first, then the
brightest or white touches, and from these
the artist works down to the most degraded tones. When the work is somewhat
advanced, he rubs the plate over with
printing ink, as if an impression were
about to be taken, in order to judge of the
effect; and, when it is nearly finished, he
has a proof taken in the rolling press, on
which he touches with white chalk to bring
it nearer to the original, and then finishes
his plate from the proof so corrected. This
mode of engraving has been made the
vehicle of conveying to the public some
curious and not unimportant experiments
with respect to colouring in pictures.

M. Le Blon, of Frankfort, entertained an
idea that all colours or tints in painting
may be exactly imitated by the three
primitive colours, either taken separately,
or mixed in various proportions. He was
aware also, that any two or more colours
passed over each other will produce a
clearer tint than the same portions of
colours mixed together and applied at
once. On these data he formed his plan,
and he has certainly succeeded in it to a
great degree, of giving printed imitations
of pictures. As his elements were the
three primitive colours, blue, red, and yellow, so he had three plates for each subject. Each plate was contrived to print
its appropriate colour, not only in the true
tones, where it was to appear pure, but also
to print, in other parts, just so much of its colour as was required of that kind of colour,

to make the compound tints, in conjunction with those proportions of the other
two colours which were given, either before or after, by means of the other plates.
This, it must be allowed, was a matter of
very difficult calculation; but his success
in the endeavour was greatly beyond ex-
pectation, and I should consider it in many
respects preferable to the present practice
of printing various colours from the same
plate; because, in the former case, the
degree of colour is determined by the
artist, who is doubtless a man of some
science; and, in the latter case, it is left to
the printer, who, in all probability, is a
man of no science at all.   The tools of
the mezzotinto engraver, in addition to
those of the engraver in lines, are two or
three kinds of scrapers, and the grounding
tools.

Etching next becomes the object of our consideration, and well does it deserve our respect and most serious attention. It has furnished to *engraving* the most powerful of all its auxiliaries; it is more masterly than any other mode of operating upon copper; it furnishes ample means for the bold and daring enterprizes of taste; and, though less finished, it is also less mechanical than the best exertions of the engraver. Who was the inventor of this process is not at present ascertainable; but the earliest specimen that we have of it is in a print, by Albert Durer, called, for distinction, the cannon. The principle on which it is performed, is to cover the copper plate with some kind of resinous or bituminous material, called a ground, and then to pierce that material through with some pointed instrument, in the re-

required forms, so that the copper, in those parts, shall be exposed to the action of a corrosive fluid, subsequently to be applied, which will in no way touch those other parts that are covered by the ground. I shall be somewhat minute in what relates to this mode of engraving, because it is a fit practice for those ladies and gentlemen who may wish to have the means of multiplying their elegant conceptions for the purpose of obliging their friends. More than one accomplished female in that august family which guides the destiny of these kingdoms, has practised etching to a considerable extent; and a lady of high rank has recently gratified her friends by some beautiful etchings after her own drawings, taken during a tour in Scotland. The ground commonly used for covering the plates is composed of

c c

four parts of virgin wax, two parts of
asphaltum, one part of amber, and one
gum-mastic, melted slowly together, and
then poured into warm water, to harden
gradually as the water cools. This ground
must be made up into small balls, and tied
in thin silk for use. The plate to receive
the ground must be heated so that the
finger will not bear to touch it, and the
ball of ground must be rubbed gently over
it, till the heat of the plate shall have
drawn so much through the silk as will
cover the whole thinly. It must then be
dabbed lightly over with a ball of cotton
tied up in silk, to distribute the ground
equally; and, when cooled, it must be
smoked entirely with the flame of a large
candle, till the whole is black, and yet
glossy : it is then ready to receive the intended subject, which may be thus accom-

plished.   The engraver makes an outline with black-lead from his original, on smooth paper, distinguishing all the small lights, and the extent of all the shadows. This being sent to the copper-plate printer, is damped and laid face downwards, on the proper part of the grounded plate ; after which, by passing it through the press, the black-lead drawing is left distinctly on the plate.   I will not take up your time this morning in stating to you the great difficulty which the engraver, who is. not a correct draftsman, encounters when his original is of a different size from that which he is to represent it.

The artist now commences his operation with the point or. etching-needle, which must be of different degrees of sharpness, according to the size of line that is intended to be given in the various parts of the work; it is even a frequent practice, in the foreground parts of large landscape subjects, to double the lines so near to each other, that they may spread into one by the subsequent action of the corroding medium. Oval-pointed needles have been used by many for the purpose of making broad lines, but they are liable to many objections, and are now, I believe, little employed. When the subject has been gone through by the artist, he must surround the plate by a kind of border, or wall, composed of bees'-wax, softened with Venice-turpentine, made with a sort of spout at one corner. The aquafortis is then to be applied, properly diluted with water, and must be half or three quarters of an inch deep on the plate. The exact proportion of water to the quantity of nitrous spirit, is a matter of difficulty depending on experience. It is used differently by different engravers, and even of different strengths, by the same engraver, for various parts of his work. The texture of one piece of copper, compared to another, will require an alteration in the power of the aquafortis, and the temperature of the room will also affect it considerably. When the faintest, or more delicate parts, are so coroded as to be judged sufficiently dark, the aquafortis must be poured off by the spout, the plate washed clean with water, and then dried; after which these faint parts must be secured by a covering of turpentine-varnish and lamp black, and the spirit applied again to act upon the remaining parts of the subject. This proceeding may be repeated, to give different degrees of dark, at the option of the artist, and the mode of so

securing the lines or objects not again to
be acted upon, is technically called *stopping out :* the corroding with the aquafortis
is also called *biting in.* The early specimens of this art appear to me to have
been corroded alike in every part, and
where there is in them a difference · of
force in the lines, it seems to have been
made by a greater or less pressure on the
point in etching. The artist, too, even
for a century after the first discovery, had
a much less convenient mode of applying
the aquafortis than that which is used at
present. He had a large tin trough, or
cistern, well pitched over the inside, at
the end of which the etched plate was
placed, in a sloping direction. He then
took his aquafortis, undiluted, in a jug or
ewer, and poured it down the plate in a
gradual stream, till the stock was ex-

17

hausted; after which the contents of the cistern were delivered into the jug, the plate turned with a different edge downwards, and the former operation repeated, till the required degree of dark had been obtained.

For a long time etching was looked on by those who practised it, merely as an expeditious mode of imitating the work of the engraver, and it was not till near our own times that the happy espousals of these two arts were solemnized. The beautiful progeny which they have since given to the world in different kingdoms, but particularly in Britain, should make us regard the union as having conferred an inestimable blessing on human society. Etching now furnishes the indispensable preparation for every subject, and is subsequently finished with the graver, the

artist allowing the one or the other to
prevail in different parts of his work, according as he may conceive its characteristic properties to suit the object he has
to express.   Respecting the proportion
which the quantity of etching in a plate
should bear to the quantity of engraving,
artists have differed very materially in
their opinions, and consequently in their
practice.   Some have left the flesh of
their figures entirely for the graver, etching a considerable part of the draperies;
some have etched also a considerable part
of the flesh in their subjects, and some
have left the figures wholly to be executed
with the graver.   Sir Robert Strange, in
many respects as fine an engraver as ever
existed, etched a great part of the work
even in the lights of his most delicate flesh.
We find, in his works, frequently a second

and even a third line in such cases, laid in
different degrees of intersection. This, no
doubt, must have been a great cause of
expediting his work, and may, probably,
succeed well in such large figures as he
generally engraved; but it seems to have
been the practice of Mr. Woollett, a name
no less distinguished in the art, to leave
his figures, which were usually of a smaller
size, to be worked out with the graver. My
time will not allow me to go more minutely into this part of the subject; yet I
must state to you that it is the opinion of
a very eminent professor of this art, whom
I have lately consulted on the subject, that
in the time of Strange, the practice of etching was introduced too much, and that in
the present times, it is probably employed
too little. I cannot help taking this opportunity to acquaint you that I have met

with the most liberal dispositions in the professors of engraving, to whom I have applied for information and assistance on your account. If my discourse of this morning should afford you instruction or amusement, the praise is wholly theirs.

There is a species of etching, of modern discovery, which I wish much to describe and recommend to you: it is called *etching in soft ground,* and is intended to imitate and multiply the effects of drawing with chalk or black-lead pencil. You will recollect that the surface of all paper is granulated, more or less, according to its fabric ; that a crayon of any kind, drawn lightly across a paper, comes in contact with only a few of the higher grains of the surface, and consequently makes what appears a faint line ; and that if the crayon be pressed forcibly down, in making a line,

it comes in contact with a greater number
of points in the surface, thus leaving the
appearance of a darker line, by its being
less divided into grains.

On this principle the etching in soft-
ground is affected.   The ground to be
used is the common etching-ground,
melted with one-third the quantity of
fine mutton suet, and it is to be laid on,
dabbed, and smoked precisely as I have
described already.   This being done, the
subject must be drawn with a small brush
and some flake-white on the thinnest
bank-post paper that can be procured ; the
paper must then be damped at the back,
and stretched over the plate, fastening it
on the back of the copper with wafers.
When dry, it becomes quite tight, and is
ready to work on.   For this purpose you
will take a hard black-lead pencil, and

draw over your subject, as you have already
indicated it by the white lines, shadowing
it freely, and just as you would make a
drawing, if there were no plate under
your paper. In proportion to the pressure
you have given to your pencil, the corres-
ponding grains of the other surface of the
paper will have been brought in contact
with the varnish or ground on the plate,
and the paper attaches so strongly as,
when removed, to bring away with it the
ground in every such point or grain. The
aquafortis is then to be applied, in the
usual mode, and the result will be a most
correct imitation of such drawing. When
I consider how very complete this process
is, in producing the end it has in view, I
cannot but regret that it was not known to
the painters of the fifteenth and sixteenth
centuries, who would thus have been

enabled to give us their conceptions of beautiful forms, without trusting them to the intervention of another, who, perhaps, did not feel, and therefore could not express, the delicate original. But I cannot quit the subject of etching, without describing to you a practice which is of high importance to every mode of engraving on plates of metal. It is professionally called *re-biting*, and consists of deepening and enlarging, by means of aquafortis, the cavities that have been made already in the plate. It is commonly effected by heating the copper, and then taking the dabber, on which some portion of the etching ground has been left by former use, and patting it lightly over the surface till the whole be covered, leaving the cavities or lines untouched. The aquafortis may then be applied to darken the whole or any part of the work ; and, also, by making new scratches or punctures with the etching needle, other work may be added to that already given before. This valuable invention is entirely English : it was first practised by Mr. Anthony Walker, who communicated it to Mr. Woollett ; and it doubtless contributed greatly to those beautiful effects which are so universally admired in his performances. But at that time the risk of filling up the finer parts of the work was considered so great, that it was not attempted without fear and trembling. It is now a common practice of the art, even in the mode I have described ; but some ingenious engravers have found means to diminish the risk. The only one which I shall describe is thus: take ten parts of common starch, to two parts of pearl-ash, and

mix them with as much gum-arabic water
as will bring the whole to the consistency
of a printing-ink. Fill the cavities of the
work with this material, taking care to
clear it perfectly from the surface of the
plate, and then apply the dabber as before
described, and without fear. When the
whole is dry, immerse the plate in
water. The starch and gum in the cavities will swell by the moisture, and burst
up the ground, if anywhere it should have
chanced to cover the lines, and the alkali,
now set at liberty, and being by nature a
dissolvent of the ground, will greatly facilitate the intention.

The next mode of engraving, which I
would wish to describe to you, is that of
aquatinta, so called from its giving the
appearance of drawings tinted with
water-colours. The first who practised
this species of art with tolerable success

was an engraver of Paris, named Le Prince,
from whom Mr. Grenville purchased the
secret, and, on his return to England, presented it sealed to Mr. Paul Sandby.   It
is a peculiarity in the history of this process, that it was discovered and brought
to perfection almost at the same time;
for Mr. Sandby was only the second
practitioner, and his works in aquatinta
are equal to any thing of the kind that
has ever been produced.   The best
method of this practice now known is
thus: — The plate being perfectly clean,
and the outline of your subject carefully
etched with the soft ground, take a solution of rosin or fine Burgundy pitch in
pure spirit of wine, of the consistency of
milk, and pour it on the plate, so as to
cover the whole surface.   Pour the surplus of this liquid immediately away, and

then keep turning the plate slowly. round upon your hand in a somewhat in-clined direction for near a quarter of an hour. During this time, the spirit of wine evaporates, and the resinous gum, not being in quantity sufficient to cover the extent of copper, cracks and splits all over into minute parts with great uniformity and exactness. These cracks, which may be made so small as not to be perceived without a glass, admit the action of the aquafortis, and, when *bit in*, form what is called the grain of the work. You will then take flake white mixed with turpentine varnish to the appearance of milk and water, which you will apply with a hair pencil to those touches that are to be left white, and, having bordered the plate with a wall, you will apply the aquafortis, considerably diluted,

D D

till it shall have given to the copper the
tone of your lightest tint.   You will then
take off the nitrous acid, dry the plate,
and repeat the operation for the different
degrees of light successively.   It is usual
amongst engravers of this class to perform the *stopping out* for the lights
with lamp-black and varnish; but the
white is better, because by keeping it
semi-transparent, it allows you to see
the effect of your work as you proceed,
which, in the other case, is entirely a
matter of conjecture.   When the smaller
lights are thus made, and where the
touch or pencilling becomes rather an
affair of dark than light, you will employ
a mixture of vermilion with strong gum-
arabic water, and paint in your objects
on the *ground*, which remains, through
the whole work, and, when that is dry,

cover the whole plate over with a thin
composition of lamp-black and turpentine varnish. As soon as this covering
seems to have a thin skin on the whole
surface, plunge the plate in water, and in
a short time the vermilion will swell,
burst up the covering which you passed
over it, and leave the form of every
touch ready to be acted upon by the
corroding menstruum. The succeeding
darks must be formed in the same manner; and, if the plate be successfully performed, the appearance is peculiar and
most beautiful. Besides, it is an advantage greatly in favour of this mode of
working in copper, that it is almost as
expeditious as drawing.

The last mode of employing the engraver's implements which I shall describe
to you, is that of working entirely in dots

or points. I speak of this the last, only because its general adoption was subsequent to that of the other modes. The practice, however, of executing the faces and other parts of plates in dots, seems to have been admitted almost as early as the manner of engraving in lines. Agostino Demusis, a pupil of Marc Antonio, has left some plates in which the flesh is worked entirely in dots; and there is a print by Giulio Campagnola, executed about the year 1516, in which the back-ground, as well as other parts, is dotted or stippled. But this manner of engraving has lately been distinguished by the name of the *chalk manner*, because about fifty years ago it was first applied to the purpose of imitating slight drawings in chalk, by De Marteau of Paris. The ingenious, but unfortunate, Mr. Ryland introduced it into this country, and Mr. Bartolozzi, whose talents were equal to any undertaking, having shown the beauty of which such a process was capable, effected its complete establishment amongst us. The dotted manner, like that of engraving in lines, is begun by etching, and is finished by the graver, though not always without the assistance of re-biting to deepen or enlarge the punctures. Many artists in this department leave the flesh of their figures to be performed wholly with the graver, but theirs is not an universal practice. The grain, by which the tones in this kind of work are produced, may be made open or close, fine and delicate, or coarse and rough, at the option of the operator, and is therefore capable of great variety. The skilful exercise of this manner in the imitations of the human figure, which we have lately witnessed in many instances, serve to show that in some respects it has powers not inferior to any other mode of engraving whatever; but, like engraving in mezzotinto, it is not well suited to a free and tasteful expression of the minute forms in landscape; nor can it, without extreme difficulty, produce a light, even tint of any extent, which, in the line manner of working, is so easily effected by the etching-needle, and the ruler.

Having thus described, concisely, the different modes of engraving, except that of Ugo da Carpi, which, as it ranks little above the stamping of paper for rooms, I did not conceive worthy your notice; I shall proceed to examine the powers of those modes towards obtaining their ultimate object. It will, I trust, be admitted,

after what I have stated to-day, that en+
graving is an imitation of painting; but
if the laudable ambition of the professors,
to give high rank to their art, should
even insist that it is, independently, an
imitation of nature, I will not dispute
their opinion: the principles by which I
mean to measure its power will still have
the same application.

First, I would wish to establish in your
minds, that there are no lines, dots, or
hatches in the surfaces of objects in nature, that there are, or should be, no such
in painting, and that such indications,
when employed, are the *means*, not the
end, of art. I would wish to remind you,
that a print, to be viewed as an imitation
either of painting or of nature, must be
placed at a distance that conceals the
means by which the effect is produced,

that, consequently, it is of little importance, whether the means employed be
lines, dots, or hatches, unless it can be
shown that *one* affords greater facilities
than the others in obtaining the ultimate
object of the art. I would next wish to
establish in your minds that no imitation
of nature, either in painting or engraving,
can have the apparent force and round-
ness of natural objects ; because it can
neither be so dark or so light where required. It will be evident to you, that a
surface, generally covered with black, if
divided ever so minutely by lines or
punctures of white, is in its general tone
rendered lighter by the division, which,
consequently tends to abridge the means
of imitation on the side of dark, in proportion as it is greater or less ; and that
that process has the most powerful means

which is least subject to such divisions. You will also admit as a fact, because it can be proved to you, that a white surface, divided by lines, dots, or hatches, cannot show so small a difference between a very faint tint, and a small white spot surrounded by it, as can be shown by a smooth colour, nor can it show the difference between one delicate tone and another, that may easily be shown by a surface not granulated or divided. Hence it will appear to you, that the more minute the means employed by the engraver in dividing the surface of the copper to express his tones, the more ample becomes his power to imitate.

These principles, which I conceive to be incontrovertible, will furnish you with the means of measuring how far each mode of engraving is qualified to attain

the great object that all have in view.
The result of such examination, candidly
and judiciously made, I have no doubt
would be, that engraving in the line
manner is more extensive than any other
manner in its means of representing
various objects, and that it is, when suc-
sessful, more meritorious than any other,
because *more difficult*, as it employs means
less congenial to the end proposed;
means which, in the practical acquirement to any degree of excellence, require
the entire devotion of those years which
should be partly employed in acquiring
principles of science; without which,
manual dexterity is nothing. Engraving
in lines, too, is I believe the most tedious
of all modes of engraving.

The practice of working in mezzotinto
is liable, from its nature, to one serious

objection, which is, that the more the
ground is scraped away, to show the
lightest tones, the coarser and more evident is the granulation made by the
grounding tool; but in those instances
where this defect has been corrected by a
delicate application of the needle, or
other pointed instrument, I am persuaded
you will readily allow them to exhibit
the most perfect examples of engraving
that have ever been produced. The
mechanical operation of engraving in
mezzotinto is so easy, that it may be
practised to a certain degree by any one,
and therefore the success which attends
its best operations is matter of science
only. It is, however, as I have stated
before, very limited, as to the kinds of
subject it is capable of treating successfully. The dotted, or stippled manner,

possesses, in light and delicate objects, some advantages over every other process of engraving. It has, in common with the line manner, that deficiency of dark which is so powerful an aid to mezzo-tinto; but, by mixing it partially with strokes, it is more general in its application to different subjects.

But whatever difference of opinion may exist amongst artists, or amongst *critics* in art, respecting the comparative merits of those processes which I have described and compared, there can be *no* difference of opinion amongst any set of men, as to the great and extensive benefits, which the art of *engraving in its various opera-tions* HAS conferred, and is still able to *confer*, upon mankind.

LECTURE VIII.

―――

In preparing this course of lectures for
your amusement and information, I felt
that I had a great and important object to
accomplish. I had undertaken to discuss
the principles and the practices of three
distinct arts, similar in their object, but
materially different in their means of obtaining it, yet all contributing by their
results to the prosperity of the empire.
It will certainly appear to you, as it appeared to me, that eight hours are a very
short time for such a discussion. How-

ever, such being the time allotted me, and
my anxious wish being to make you correct judges at least, if not practitioners in
those arts, I was under the necessity of
adopting such a plan, as would bring my
indispensable materials into the smallest
possible compass.   For this purpose, I
began the course, by endeavouring to establish general principles : my next object
was to show their just application, and,
through the whole, to adopt a logical mode
of arrangement, that whatever was proved
in one lecture, or admitted by definition,
might become the ground of subsequent
deduction and further reasoning; making
the whole a regular series of axioms, definitions and demonstrations.   But requisite as this kind of arrangement was, on
account of the great extent of my subject,
it has been necessarily attended by the dis-

18

advantage that will arise on such occasions,
to a fluctuating and variable auditory.
Those, it is true, who did me the honour
to attend my first lecture, would be convinced that I was not going to mislead
them, and might still, I trust, continue in
the same opinion, if they had opportunity
to hear the whole course ; but those casual
visitors who, from other engagements,
could hear only one lecture or part of a
lecture now and then, may, perhaps, by
losing the connection of general reasoning
which I wished to preserve, have been led
to doubt my correctness in some points.
On this account, I have judged it most
proper to employ the last hour that remains to me, in a recapitulation of the
arguments, practices and demonstrations,
introduced in the preceding lectures, and
I am extremely solicitous to impress them

on your minds, that you may hereafter become the judicious patrons of those arts so connected with the prosperity of our country.

Drawing, or the representation of forms by lines, has been the first object of our consideration in the discussion of these arts. Taken even generally, it is of high importance in human affairs, since it fixes distinctly in the mind of each practitioner the perception of such figures as it leads him to contemplate, and may therefore be employed as an useful auxiliary in almost every branch of education. But to the painter, the practice of drawing is indispensable, as the only means by which he can fill his mind with a perfect knowledge of those objects, out of which he is to combine his future pictures, and it is indispensable to him in correctly express-

ing the objects for his picture when selected from the storehouse of his mind.
Thus, then, to *paint* also implies to *draw*,
and that in such way as will conduce most
to perfect representation.   This great end,
I have shown you, cannot be obtained by
careless and slovenly drawing, so common
in these times : for the forms that have
been drawn will be retained by the mind,
in exact proportion to the accuracy
of the delineation.   Drawing, as far as
it expresses contours or dimensions of
forms, should be executed in a single,
distinct, and steady line, taking each part
at one motion of the hand, to the extent
that the hand will move freely, and all
retouching of the lines must be rejected.
If an incorrectness appear, the part must
be erased, and a new line made as clear
and decided as the first, but more true.

E E

This mode of drawing was held as the criterion of excellence amongst the ancient Greek painters ; and I am persuaded, the anecdote related by Pliny, of Apelles and Protogenes, was no more than a trial of manual skill, which could draw the finest and most even line. Since the revival of the arts in modern times, the same opinion has prevailed on this point; for we find that Giotto, the immediate successor of Cimabue, was chosen, in preference to other painters, to decorate the papal palace, because he could draw a perfect circle with one motion of his hand. I wish most anxiously to fix this in your minds.

To drawing belong, *proportion* and *expression*. For the first you may take, as general guides, the dimensions prescribed by Polignotus for the various parts of the human figure, and which were held in such esteem .by the Greeks, that they were, emphatically called the. *rule*. But they will serve you only as general guides; because.they are not all to be found in any one human being, and the most cele- brated statues of *those very Greeks* deviate very considerably and variously in many examples from the *rule* of Polignotus. In studying expression, so far as it relates to the evidences of inward feeling and passion, I have advised you to consult the Treatise of Gerrarde Lairesse, and Mr. Bell's elegant work on the anatomy of expression in painting : your own ob- servations, too, made in the daily inter- course with your friends and intimates, will show you at least the manner of pourtraying every kind of amiable feeling. But when your subjects require to depict those passions and intentions which con-

nect themselves with *motion*, you must
endeavour to obtain some knowledge of
the structure and workings of the human
frame. In this, as I have shown you in a
former lecture, the statues of antiquity will
afford you little assistance. They are
frequently incorrect in the forms and
places of the muscles. You must, therefore, for this purpose, have recourse to engravings of anatomical subjects, of which
there are many good ones that can
be easily procured. But the greatest
difficulty you will have to encounter in
the practice of drawing is, when the objects you wish to represent are in such a
position as to be what painters call fore-
shortened, and which happens in a greater
or less degree in some part of almost
every figure. Here rules, as applied
to the human figure, are of little or
no use. I would advise you, therefore,

to practise this at every opportunity; because it will give you, subsequently, great power and facility in expressing varieties of forms. The particular cases in which the fore-shortening of whole figures may be allowed, and even must be adopted, are those in which *one* is to appear of much greater relative extent, with regard to the other objects in your picture, than you can afford it, without detriment to the seeming consequence of the other figures ; and again in the painting of subjects for ceilings. It is not uncommon, even in this country, to see in the ceilings of elegant and tasteful apartments, nymphs, cupids, and all kinds of figures, sporting in shady groves or on verdant plains ; and the spectator, seeing that they are all horizontal, has a sensation as if they were likely to fall down upon his head. The subjects for these purposes should always be represented as if placed at a considerable degree of elevation, and as if seen from below. The perspective plane of the picture then becomes parallel to the plane of the horizon, and the figures, or other objects intended to appear as standing upright, must be fore-shortened or diminished from the base towards a point of sight, as, in the common practices of perspective, the horizontal dimensions are fore-shortened. This, however, *has been*, or probably will be, demonstrated to you by your lecturer on perspective, and therefore requires no further explanation from me; but for examples of this kind of fore-shortening, I would refer you to the different ceilings painted by Rubens, which are drawn with great ability. *Drawing* or *outline*, as applied to landscape, should be equally clear, correct, and decided, giving the characteristic expression of each object and material, and constantly marking by a different strength of line, the comparative recession of each succeeding distance. But care must be taken that, after representing correctly the details of the near objects, you do not insert the same details in those distant objects, in which they would not be discernible. This error, from your knowledge of the parts, you will be very liable to commit, and should therefore guard yourselves against it.

To mere outline have been added, by various practitioners, many auxiliaries, with a view to approach nearer to the representation of nature; but in these the outline always makes an evident part, and is the characteristic distinction between

E E 4

Drawing and *Painting*. There is no one of those modes, perhaps, more delightful to the artist, or pleasing to the spectator, than *that* of tinted drawing. The process of this mode, I have shown you, consists in giving the light and shadow of your subject with Indian ink,* and then staining it with the local colours and the colours of the reflections. I would advise this for the first practice of all who wish to become proficients in painting.

Painting has probably been practised by one nation or another for three thousand years, and during two thousand seven hundred years of that time its operations have been carried on in water-

* Indian ink is invariably recommended on these occasions, because it fixes itself in the paper, and because it gives a deeper tone with less substance of colour than any other material at present known.

colours of two kinds, fresco and distemper.
Neither of these modes, I have shown,
would be desirable for you to adopt, and
you are therefore left to exercise your
taste in the modern practice of oil-colours,
or in the still more modern practice of
transparent water-colours on white paper.
It was my duty to prove to you in the
early part of these lectures, that oil-colours
are not permanent, and that the others
are permanent, almost without exception;
but as the possibility with thick colours
of covering the work *repeatedly*, enables
the practitioner to correct or conceal
blunders; the use of oil-colours will continue to have its advocates, notwithstanding the greater neatness and superior
force of pictures in water-colours. I have
given you, therefore, the best rules of
practice for each mode, derived either
from the works of eminent masters, or

from philosophical principles; and I advise you to admit no one proceeding whatever into your drawings or pictures, unless you can show, by correct reasoning, that it will lead, by the shortest way, to the end you have in view, which is the imitation of well-selected nature.

Your works in oil-colours should be always executed on a white ground, and the more thinly you paint them, the longer they will continue nearly of the colour they appear when first completed. In *water-colours*, you will begin by supposing the objects you have to represent as being all white, and then, the outline being correctly made, you will shadow with Indian ink the objects or parts of objects that are turned from the light, or from which the light is intercepted by other objects. You will then, with the same material, express in your work the various degrees of light on the surfaces left in light by the first proceeding. You are then prepared to consider your objects in nature as coloured, and must proceed with transparent pigments to give the local colours in your work, and the compound colours occasioned by the reflections from surrounding surfaces. You will then finish the shadowed parts with a mixture of the appropriate local colours and Indian ink. The result of this proceeding, even in moderately skilful hands, must be successful; because it can be proved that the process is precisely the same as that by which the phenomena of objects in nature are produced, and consequently, even with the most clumsy practitioner, it can produce nothing very bad. These points I have demonstrated to you already.

But having chosen your mode of painting, and perfected the outline of your subject, whatever it be, (I speak of original compositions,) your next consideration is to distribute the light and shadow, so that taste, as well as truth, may be satisfied. Your quantity of bright light should be equal to a quarter of the picture, and this should be distributed into three masses, irregularly placed; of which the principal or chief light should take a half of one-eighth, or a sixteenth, of the whole picture, the second light should occupy two-thirds of what remains, and the smallest portion should be given to the third remainder. My object being now merely to recapitulate, I give you the rules without the reasoning on which I have shown them to be founded. If your subject be of figures, the most important of those must receive the chief light; if it be of landscape, the chief light in general will be in the sky, the second on some part of the the fore-ground, and the. third in the water, if any appear, or on the figures, for the purpose of distributing the tones and colours of the sky. The quantity of extreme dark in your pictures should be equal to one-fourth the extent of surface, and the simi-tones, or reflected lights, should occupy the remaining space, or one half of the whole.

Having reviewed the principles and rules by which you are to arrange the light and shadow of your pictures, the next consideration is the *colouring*, and an important object of consideration most truly it is, involving, in a great measure, the nature of the first impression which your picture will make on the spectator.

Colouring we have already *understood*

as being a matter of pure imitation, and
again as being a matter of arrangement
or combination ; and we have also understood that the objects for imitation should
be so chosen, and afterwards so placed in
a picture that a strict compliance with
the rules for arrangement of colours
should require nothing incompatible with
the strictest truth of representation. The
proper maxims to guide you in both cases,
and in different processes, I have already
given you, and shall now, therefore, only
recal to your memories the chief points
of them. In landscape, you will begin
with the blue expanse of the sky, then
proceed to the light clouds, and their grey
shadows. The distance then becomes
the object of your attention, constantly
introducing so much of the blue or grey
of the sky into its shadows, as well as into

14

those of the near parts, as will represent
the effect of atmosphere counteracting the
darkness. You will invariably make your
greens in landscape, of brown, blue, and
yellow, wherever transparent greens áre
required, and also with the addition of
white, when the foliage should, from the
nature of your process, be expressed with
opaque materials. If your pictures be of
figures, the great difficulty you have to
encounter in the colouring is that of expressing truly the grey or violet-coloured
tints. These are of two kinds, — where the
veins show through the thinness of the
skin, which are called local, and those
which appear at the edges of the shadows
of the first class, and are called accidental,
as depending on the direction of light.
In *oils*, these tints are to be expressed
with blue, red, and white; with red, black,

and white; or with black and white, according to the complexion. They must be inserted of a strong tone, and glazed down, in the subsequent stages of the picture, with simi-transparent flesh-colours, till the requisite degree of delicacy be obtained. In *water-colours* of a large size on paper these grey tints will be expressed with Antwerp or Prussian blue and carmine; in miniature-painting on ivory, they must be expressed with ultramarine, or ultramarine and vermilion. In the arrangement of your colours I have had the honour to show you that white and yellow should make your centre, occupying, with the addition of some portion of red, the chief mass of light prescribed in the discussion of tones. To these must succeed the purple, blue, and green; but it should be remembered that the white of the

centre must be contrasted by some portion
of dark, and that each mass of colour
must also have, in its immediate neighbourhood, some indications of its opposite
kind of colour.

There is perhaps no instance of a more
masterly management of these points, than
may be found in the picture, by Nicolo
Poussin, of the last supper, in the mag-
nificent collection at Cleveland-house. The
noble proprietor has most patriotically
opened his house once a year to public in-
spection; I cannot refer you to a better
school for acquiring the various excellen-
cies I have described in these lectures,
than you will find in those splendid gal-
leries. I have said little or nothing in
these lectures, on the practice of painting
in crayons. The process has certainly
some beauties, but its productions are so

perishable in their nature, even by the most trifling accidents, and so fugitive in their appearance, that I have no hesitation in giving my opinion that the use of crayons, for producing *pictures*, should be positively rejected by all who wish their *performances* to continue beyond the duration of a few weeks. I have also avoided to say much of the practice of *drawing* in black and white chalk upon coloured paper; because, when carried to its utmost perfection, it leads no further in the progress towards painting, and because, from the facility it gives of making masses of light and dark, it seems to do much, and yet gains almost nothing. I am convinced it ought to be rejected and prohibited in our national school of arts, and the plan I have recommended, of drawing and shading in lines, according to the per-

spective direction of the surface; substituted in its place. Till this shall have
been done, the English school, I dare venture to say, will never be esteemed for its
correctness in the expression of forms.

Having thus deliberately viewed, and
slightly reviewed the principles, the practices, and the powers of different modes
of drawing and painting, allow me to entreat that you will now look on them, as
the means of promoting your amusement,
your knowledge, your happiness. If you
journey through our own delightful country to impress your minds patriotically
with a consciousness of its unrivalled beauties; if you travel to foreign lands, to examine their wonders, either of nature or
art, you will find the practice of drawing,
almost indispensable to those ends. Forms
of any kind looked on, even with enthu-

siasm, leave but a vague impression on
the memory, and daily experience convinces us how very inadequate verbal description is, to convey notions of shapes and
colours; but by means of the pencil you will
not only fix indelibly in your thoughts, the
objects you wish to retain, but you will
also supply yourselves with the delightful
means of communicating to your friends,
and to others, that information which
probably .without *you,* they might never
have the opportunity to procure. To such
as are engaged in the military profession,
prompt and accurate drawing is of the
. highest importance, as furnishing the
means of retaining, or of conveying to
others engaged in the same pursuit, the
most useful intelligence, by which, in some
cases, even hundreds of lives may be
saved. In the practice of painting, you

will not find less gratifying rewards for
your labours. If you undertake subjects
of history, you will be led more closely
to examine and to understand the characters of the personages you introduce, and
thus perhaps to draw conclusions, which
would not otherwise have occurred to you;
besides the very valuable benefit of fix-
ing those transactions inexpugnably in
your minds.   You will, also, in this pursuit, be led to investigate the customs, the '
manners, and the dresses of different ages
and nations, and I am persuaded that the
purposes of historical and classical reading
would invariably be best obtained by connecting them, as a part of education, with
the practice of drawing and painting.   If
you engage yourselves in the study of portraiture, your hearts will immediately point
out to you how intimately it is connected

with our dearest interests, with our most
gratifying sympathies. You will be able
to give an additional charm to your domestic apartments, by hanging round them
the faithful resemblances of your absent
friends, and even to hold seeming converse
with those whom the hand of death has
snatched from you for ever. But besides
these most refined *gratifications to yourselves,* a talent for portrait-painting, duly
exerted, will afford you the further *satisfaction* of administering in the same degree to the enjoyment of others who have
not made the same advances in art. If
you devote your leisure to the *painting* of
landscape, and in doing *that* will pursue
the advice I have so repeatedly given, you
will be enabled to enjoy for years, the picturesque beauties of countries and places
long since visited, and will retrace with

delight, each lawn, each shade, which circumstances have rendered dear to memory.
You will also, if proficients in landscape-
painting, have the power to create round
your apartments, the beauties of every
clime, of every season, whatever be that
which prevails without your walls.

Let me entreat such of you as are not
already engaged in some of these pursuits, and have yet leisure for them, to
delay no longer taking up the pencil, the
palette, or the graver. It is indispensable
to comfort, it is necessary to happiness,
that we should be furnished constantly
with the means of such employments as
will fully engage the faculties of our
minds, and at the same time greatly interest our wishes for the result. This is
to be found, perhaps, only in the practice
of the imitative arts; for in *these*, the most

consummate master is never quite certain
as to what degree of success will attend
his labours. To the youthful and gay,
I would recommend these studies most
particularly : they furnish preventions
for that lassitude which so often arises
amongst persons of fortune from want of
employment, and thus, in many cases,
they become the fortunate substitutes for
dangerous dissipations. But if it should
be said that such employments are suited
only to the young and the cheerful, whose
minds and fingers are pliant, I will answer, that the suggestion may hold good
against taking up the practice of music at
a late period, but that drawing, painting, and engraving, which are chiefly
efforts of mind, proving every step of its
operations as it proceeds; the more the
mind of the student is matured, the more

rapid will be his advancement. Polidoro da Caravaggio was five-and-twenty before he touched a pencil of any kind, and we know what his practice was in the ulti-mate.

I would now entreat your indulgence and attention while we consider these three arts in another, and perhaps not less important, relation to our interests. This is in the influence they have, and will probably long continue to have, on the prosperity of our commerce, and conse-quently on our national strength and in-dependence.

In ancient times, when sculpture flou-rished amongst the states of Greece, their superstitious worship of idols carried the efforts of the chisel to very great excellence. There could be no motive more calculated to excite enthusiastic exertion, than the wish *adequately* to represent the persons of supposed deities; nor could there be any more stimulating *reward* than that *veneration*, which the multitude constantly paid to the *artists* who *created* the deities they were taught to believe omnipotent: he who could create a divinity must himself be little less than divine. In succeeding ages, after the worship of the true God had banished idols from the sacred temples of religion, the superstitions of papacy, which long overclouded the brightening hemisphere, substituted the efforts of the pencil for those of the chisel, and the same causes soon led to the same effects in favour of the other art. In this country, at present, the arts of painting and sculpture are acknowledged to be in a low state compared with those former

instances, nor could it well be otherwise;
since those powerful motives, those considerations to exertion, no longer exist.
Let us then try to give to the professors
of art an inducement equally powerful;
let us endeavour anxiously to facilitate
its operation, and the result, we cannot
doubt it, will be as glorious as the most
sanguine could desire.

The noble, the predominant feeling in
the bosom of every Briton, is an ardent
love of the country which gave him birth.
Let it then be shown to our native artists
that the wealth, the happiness, the dignified rank of the country, depend on
their successful labours, and we shall have
furnished them with a motive that must
lead to the most brilliant successes. That
this is a fact we shall have no great difficulty to show. Our great wealth is evi-

dently the result of our flourishing commerce, the unexampled extent of that
commerce is chiefly owing to the very
great superiority of taste and design manifested in all our manufactures, and these
qualities are ramifications of those notions
in imitative art, diffused throughout the
kingdom by our national school of painting and sculpture. But though this salu-
tary and valuable effect has been produced
to a certain degree by the establishment
of the Royal Academy, its operation is
necessarily circuitous and slow; too slow
under the present circumstances of the
country. The advances that are made in
the practice of painting and sculpture in
the metropolis, being at first confined to
persons of superior talents, can only reach
the distant provinces by their general action on the public mind, and must con-

sequently be long, even years, before they
arrive at the seats of our principal manu-
factories.   I have no doubt, after this
view of the subject, you will readily perceive that if a plan could be devised for
circulating rapidly through the realm,
the true principles of imitative art, and
its constantly occurring improvements,
the beneficial effects would be immediate
and in due proportion.   For this purpose
it is that I venture to lay my ideas before
you, as a medium through which they
may be made generally known.   I would
have a school or academy immediately
established, for the instruction of two
hundred young persons in the practice
of every branch of drawing and painting, and this instruction to be given
without any fee or expence to the students.   They should be taught these arts

not only as they are complete professions of themselves, but they should likewise be taught the manner in which they connect themselves with the mechanic arts, and with manufactures. The silversmith and the chaser in metals should be enabled to acquire a knowledge of forms and decorations; the cabinet-maker should *there* learn the possibility of connecting accommodation and convenience with elegance ; the designer for printed calicoes, chintzes, and paper-hangings, should there be taught to substitute the beauties of natural objects for unmeaning arbitrary forms ; the engraver should acquire, under this establishment, that indispensable knowledge of drawing so seldom found in his profession ; and the destined painter should there commence a course of studies, founded on clear demonstration,

19

that will ensure him success in proportion to his industry.

A small annual subscription from 150 to 200 patrons would defray all the expenses of such an establishment; and, I am persuaded, there are many professed artists, in the different branches, who would take pleasure in giving their attendance and instruction gratuitously.

A hundred governors, or annual subscribers, should be admitted, to pay two guineas each for the first year, and one guinea every year afterwards, for which they should have each the privilege of sending two students each to the school, and also that of keeping them there or changing them at pleasure. When the students, who direct their views to mechanic arts, shall have accomplished themselves, they will carry the correct principles of taste and design into all their subsequent productions; when those, who soar to the higher distinctions of drawing and painting shall have finished their studies, they should be chosen by the preference of greater merit, to fill provincial stations in different parts of the kingdom, as *Drawing-masters*, to form, not to mislead, the public taste; and their introduction to such stations should be enforced by every influence in the power of those who patronise the establishment. In all such cases, I am persuaded, the country would receive such introduction as a favour conferred; for it is lamentable to see, in some of our most opulent country towns, what miserable hands are tolerated and applied to, merely because there are no others. By proper regulations made for the purpose, the subscribers might take it in

rotation, two at a time, to visit the establ-
lishment during the hours of study ; thus
preserving decorum, exciting emulation,
and gratifying, at once, their own patriotic
and tasteful feelings. But you will perhaps now think it time to enquire, whence
is to come the instruction by which these
effects are to be produced ? I answer, tha t
it should come from the voluntary attendance of the different artists of the metropolis, who should be invited to it for that
purpose by the patrons, and their visits
might be so arranged, as to become but a
very small tax on the time of any one of
them.   I dare venture to assert, that there
is no one artist of eminence in this great
city who, being fully informed of the
nature and intention of such an establishment, would hesitate a moment to give it
his cordial assistance.

I am persuaded the most beneficial effects would result from such an institution, and I trust the patriotic lovers of art will take up the subject seriously. Should such be the case, I pledge myself to assist their intentions, by furnishing a detailed plan for the purpose.

Thus, ladies and gentlemen, my duty is now nearly accomplished. For seven sessions of this most praiseworthy institution I have had the honour to appear before you as your voluntary, and gratuitous servant, in discussing the principles and practices of drawing and painting. I was induced to this undertaking by the pleasing hope, that in leading you, through philosophical principles, to a successful cultivation of those arts, I should stimulate the professors of them to emulation and industry, and thus contribute to the general prosperity. The only duty that remains for me to perform, is a most pleasing one: it is to offer you the expression of my lively gratitude for the polite attention with which you have constantly honoured me.

THE END.

LONDON:
Printed by A. & R. Spottiswoode,
New-Street-Square.

CPSIA information can be obtained at www.ICGtesting.com
Printed in the USA
270689BV00004B/90/P